Copyright @ 2021 by Isaac De-Graft Takyi
www.itdegraft.com

Published in Canada by
Quest Publications
Ontario, Canada.

Printed in Canada

Cover Design, Interior Formatting & Layout by Quest Publications
(questpublications@outlook.com)

ISBN-13: 978-1-988439-31-0

Contents

Isaac De-Graft Takyi

Dedication

To all members of Living Word Assembly of God, Toronto, Canada

and

To the body of Christ, globally.

Acknowledgement

Very grateful to God for the opportunity.

Special thanks to Pastor Cyril Opoku (Youth Pastor, Living Word A/G, Toronto) for putting this book together, Deacon Prince Donkor (Small Groups Coordinator, Living Word A/G, Toronto) for compiling the Small Group lessons, and to Joseph Osei-Amoah (Media Lead, Living Word A/G, Toronto) for all the work in putting presentation slides together for the congregational services in which these sermons were preached.

To God be all the glory!

Quotes

"For God so loved the world, that he gave his only Son, that whoever believes in him should not perish but have eternal life.

—John 3:16 ESV

And he answered, "You shall love the Lord your God with all your heart and with all your soul and with all your strength and with all your mind, and your neighbor as yourself."

—Luke 10:27

People are illogical, unreasonable, and self-centered. Love them anyway. If you do good, people will accuse you of selfish ulterior motives. Do good anyway. If you are successful, you win false friends and true enemies. Succeed anyway. The good you do today will be forgotten tomorrow. Do good anyway. Honesty and frankness make you vulnerable. Be honest and frank anyway. The biggest men with the biggest ideas can be shot down by the smallest men with the smallest minds. Think big anyway. People favor underdogs but follow only top dogs. Fight for a few underdogs anyway. What you spend years building may be destroyed overnight. Build anyway. People really need help but may attack you if you do help them. Help people anyway. Give the world the best you have, and you will get kicked in the teeth. Give the world the best you have anyway.

—Kent M. Keith "Paradoxical Commandments of Leadership".

Isaac De-Graft Takyi

Introduction

The purpose of this book is to encourage humanity to focus on making the main thing in life the main thing. What is life all about? What is the main thing in life for life? If Jesus reveals that the most important commandment is to love, it will be for our good and in our best interest to obey it.

This is the first part of the collection of the sermons on love that was preached at Living Word Assembly of God church in Toronto, Canada. Some of the sermon titles include but not limited to "THE LIFE OF LOVE: THE LOVE LIFE" which explains what love is; "THE LORD LOVES PEOPLE" revealing the focus of the Lord's love; "CHRIST THE ULTIMATE LOVE", reminding us of the sacrifice that Christ made on the Cross; "THE SPIRIT OF LOVE", the nature of the Spirit; "LOVE MAKES DISCIPLES", explaining how love obeys The Great Commission; "LOVE IS GENEROUS", teaching how love gives; and "LOVE IS GRATEFUL", showing that love's attitude is gratitude.

My joy will be to see my esteemed readers make a difference in their world through the power of their love.

1

THE LIFE OF LOVE—"THE LOVE LIFE"

"For God so loved the world, that he gave his only Son, that whoever believes in him should not perish but have eternal life.

—John 3:16 ESV

PURPOSE

The purpose is to empower us to live a life of Love with the understanding of what Love is:

1. The Love Life Is Generous
2. The Love Life Is Not Discriminatory
3. The Love Life Hates Sin
4. The Love Life Shares the Gospel Boldly in Love
5. The Love Life Forgives

The term love can be used in the narrow sense, to mean:

- The primary emotions that draw people together to form a lasting, committed relationship between them, regardless of sexual orientation.

- The commitment to fight for the highest possible good in the life of another person. In other words, **Love is the faithful and benevolent self-giving to a person.**

THE GREAT AND THE GREATEST COMMANDMENTS:

1. Old Testament References

Leviticus

18 "You shall not take vengeance or bear a grudge against the sons of your own people, but you shall love your neighbor as yourself: I am the Lord." —Leviticus 19:9-18

Deuteronomy

Hear, O Israel: The LORD our God is one LORD: And thou shalt love the LORD thy God with all thine heart, and with all thy soul, and with all thy might. —Deuteronomy 6:4-5

2. New Testament References

Matthew Henry sums up the question of which is the great commandment:

> It was a question disputed among the critics in the Law. Some would have the Law of Circumcision to be the Great Commandment, others the Law of the Sabbath, others

the Law of Sacrifices, according as they severally stood affected, and spent their zeal; now they would try what Christ said to this question, hoping to incense the people against him, if he should not answer according to the vulgar opinion; and if he should magnify one commandment, they would reflect on him as vilifying the rest.

Gospel of Matthew

And one of them, a lawyer, asked him a question to test him. "Teacher, which is the great commandment in the Law?" And he said to him, "You shall love the Lord your God with all your heart and with all your soul and with all your mind. This is the great and first commandment. And a second is like it: You shall love your neighbor as yourself. On these two commandments depend all the Law and the Prophets." —Matthew 22:35-40

Gospel of Mark

In the Gospel of Mark, the Shema is included:

And one of the scribes came up and heard them disputing with one another, and seeing that he answered them well, asked him, "Which commandment is the most important of all?" Jesus answered, "The most important is, 'Hear, O Israel: The Lord our God, the Lord is one. And you shall love the Lord your God with all your heart and with all your soul and with all your mind and with all your strength.' The second is this: 'You shall love your neighbor as

yourself.' There is no other commandment greater than these." —
Mark 12:28-31

Gospel of Luke

*And behold, a lawyer stood up to put him to the test, saying,
"Teacher, what shall I do to inherit eternal life?" He said to him,
"What is written in the Law? How do you read it?" And he
answered, "You shall love the Lord your God with all your heart
and with all your soul and with all your strength and with all your
mind, and your neighbor as yourself." And he said to him, "You
have answered correctly; do this, and you will live.* — Luke 10:25-
28

Gospel of John

*When he had gone out, Jesus said, "Now is the Son of Man
glorified, and God is glorified in him. If God is glorified in him,
God will also glorify him in himself, and glorify him at once. Little
children, yet a little while I am with you. You will seek me, and just
as I said to the Jews, so now I also say to you, 'Where I am going you
cannot come.' A new commandment I give to you, that you love one
another: just as I have loved you, you also are to love one another.
By this all people will know that you are my disciples, if you have
love for one another."* — John 13:31-35

Love Life love's God then loves people, or Love Life loves people with the love of God.

IT IS "FIRST AND GREATEST":

Adam Clarke, in his *Commentary on the Bible*, wrote:

This is the first and great commandment. It is "first and greatest":

1. In its ***antiquity***, being as old as the world, and engraved originally on our very nature.

2. In its ***dignity***; as directly and immediately proceeding from and referring to God.

3. In its ***excellence***; being the commandment of the new covenant, and the very spirit of the Divine adoption.

4. In its ***justice***, because it alone renders to God his due, prefers him before all things, and secures to him his proper rank in relation to them.

5. In its ***sufficiency***; being in itself capable of making men holy in this life, and happy in the other.

6. In its ***fruitfulness***, because it is the root of all commandments, and the fulfilling of the law.

7. In its ***virtue and efficacy***, because by this alone God reigns in the heart of humans, and humans are united to God.

8. In its **extent,** leaving nothing to the creature, which it does not refer to the Creator.

9. In its **necessity;** being absolutely indispensable.

10. In its **duration,** ever to be continued on earth, and never to be discontinued in heaven.

Scripturally:

Love is the central attribute of God, the primary fruit of the followers of God, and the defining characteristic of the kingdom of God announced in Jesus.[1] Jesus is Love, Jesus is Love Personified. Love life is Jesus, Jesus is Love Life. Love life loves God and loves People.

What does it mean to Live a Love Life, like Jesus?

A believer wants to be as much like Jesus as he or she can be. Part of being like Jesus is loving like Jesus loved. God has a goal of conforming us to the image of His Son (Romans 8:29—*For those whom he foreknew he also predestined to be conformed to the image of his Son, in order that he might be the firstborn among many brothers.*).

---

[1] Nettelhorst, R. P. (2014). *Love.* D. Mangum, D. R. Brown, R. Klippenstein, & R. Hurst (Eds.), *Lexham Theological Wordbook.* Bellingham, WA: Lexham Press.

- Jesus was always obedient to the Father (John 8:29) *"And he who sent me is with me. He has not left me alone, for I always do the things that are pleasing to him."*

- Jesus was pure in every way (Hebrews 4:15) *For we do not have a high priest who is unable to sympathize with our weaknesses, but one who in every respect has been tempted as we are, yet without sin.*

- Jesus loved people selflessly (Matthew 9:36; 14:14) *When he saw the crowds, he had compassion for them, because they were harassed and helpless, like sheep without a shepherd. When he went ashore, he saw a great crowd, and he had compassion on them and healed their sick.*

- Jesus commanded His disciples to love each other the same way He had loved them (John 13:34). *A new commandment I give to you, that you love one another: just as I have loved you, you also are to love one another.*

But that presents a problem. The truth is:

Jesus demonstrated His love by dying for us, saying, *"There is no greater love than this"* (John 15:13). *Greater love has no one than this, that someone lay down his life for his friends.*

Since most of us will never be called upon to die for someone, what does it mean to love like Jesus?

1. THE LOVE LIFE IS GENEROUS

John 3:16 tells us what it means to Live a love Life like Jesus loves: *"God so loved the world that he gave his one and only Son."*

- Godly love gives sacrificially. Loving like Jesus means we hold everything we own with loose hands, including our lives.

- We are willing to part with money, talents, time, and possessions in order to serve other people.

- We recognize that all we have is on loan to us from our Father in heaven and we are responsible for what we do with it (Matthew 25:14–30): *14 "For it will be like a man going on a journey, who called his servants and entrusted to them his property. 15 To one he gave five talents, to another two, to another one, to each according to his ability. Then he went away. 16 He who had received the five talents went at once and traded with them, and he made five talents more. 17 So also, he who had the two talents made two talents more. 18 But he who had received the one talent went and dug in the ground and hid his master's money. 19 Now after a long time the master of those servants came and settled accounts with them. 20 And he who had received the five talents came forward, bringing five talents more, saying,*

'Master, you delivered to me five talents; here, I have made five talents more.' 21 His master said to him, 'Well done, good and faithful servant. You have been faithful over a little; I will set you over much. Enter into the joy of your master.' 22 And he also who had the two talents came forward, saying, 'Master, you delivered to me two talents; here, I have made two talents more.' 23 His master said to him, 'Well done, good and faithful servant. You have been faithful over a little; I will set you over much. Enter into the joy of your master.' 24 He also who had received the one talent came forward, saying, 'Master, I knew you to be a hard man, reaping where you did not sow, and gathering where you scattered no seed, 25 so I was afraid, and I went and hid your talent in the ground. Here, you have what is yours.' 26 But his master answered him, 'You wicked and slothful servant! You knew that I reap where I have not sown and gather where I scattered no seed? 27 Then you ought to have invested my money with the bankers, and at my coming I should have received what was my own with interest. 28 So take the talent from him and give it to him who has the ten talents. 29 For to everyone who has will more be given, and he will have an abundance. But from the one who has not, even what he has will be taken away. 30 And cast the worthless servant into the outer darkness. In that place there will be weeping and gnashing of teeth.'

- We give people what they need when it is within our power to do so. When we see a brother or sister in need, and we have resources that could help, we are to share what we have with them (James 2:15-17; 1 John 3:16–17): *15 If a brother or sister is poorly clothed and lacking in daily food, 16 and one of you says to them, "Go in peace, be warmed and filled," without giving them the things needed for the body, what good is that? 17 So also faith by itself, if it does not have works, is dead. 16 By this we know love, that he laid down his life for us, and we ought to lay down our lives for the brothers. 17 But if anyone has the world's goods and sees his brother in need, yet closes his heart against him, how does God's love abide in him?*

2. THE LOVE LIFE IS UNDISCRIMINATORY

Jesus was undiscriminating in the way He loved. He warned us that it is easy to love those who are like us (Luke 6:32–33). *32 "If you love those who love you, what benefit is that to you? For even sinners love those who love them. 33 And if you do good to those who do good to you, what benefit is that to you? For even sinners do the same"*

But Jesus loved even His enemies and expects His followers to do the same (Luke 6:35). *"But love your enemies, and do good, and lend, expecting nothing in return, and your reward will be great, and you will be sons of the Most High, for he is kind to the ungrateful and the evil."*

He healed, fed, and ministered to many who would later cry, "Crucify Him!" (Matthew 27:20–22). *"Now the chief priests and the elders persuaded the crowd to ask for Barabbas and destroy Jesus. 21 The governor again said to them, "Which of the two do you want me to release for you?" And they said, "Barabbas." 22 Pilate said to them, "Then what shall I do with Jesus who is called Christ?" They all said, "Let him be crucified!"*

He washed the feet of Judas Iscariot, knowing that within hours Judas would betray Him (John 13:4–5*). "[Jesus] rose from supper. He laid aside his outer garments, and taking a towel, tied it around his waist. 5 Then he poured water into a basin and began to wash the disciples' feet and to wipe them with the towel that was wrapped around him."*

He made a point of ministering to the hated Samaritans (John 4), even making a Samaritan the hero of a parable (Luke 10:25–37): The Parable of the good Samaritan.

Rich and poor, young and old, religious and pagan—people flocked to hear Jesus because He loved them (Mark 10:1; Matthew 9:35–36; Luke 18:18).
Mark 10:1— *"And he left there and went to the region of Judea and beyond the Jordan, and crowds gathered to him again. And again, as was his custom, he taught them."*

Matthew 9:35–36: *"And Jesus went throughout all the cities and villages, teaching in their synagogues and proclaiming the gospel of the kingdom and healing every disease and every affliction. 36*

When he saw the crowds, he had compassion for them, because they were harassed and helpless, like sheep without a shepherd."

Luke 18:18—*"And a ruler asked him, "Good Teacher, what must I do to inherit eternal life?"*

To love like Jesus means we cannot be selective in how we treat people. James strongly condemns favoritism based on financial or social status: *"But if you show favoritism, you sin and are convicted by the law as transgressors"* (James 2:9). We are to treat every human being with dignity and respect, remembering that this person is a special creation, designed in the image of God (1 John 2:9–10; 4:20–21).

1 John 2:9–10: *"Whoever says he is in the light and hates his brother is still in darkness. 10 Whoever loves his brother abides in the light, and in him there is no cause for stumbling."*

1 John 4:20–21: *"If anyone says, "I love God," and hates his brother, he is a liar; for he who does not love his brother whom he has seen cannot love God whom he has not seen. 21 And this commandment we have from him: whoever loves God must also love his brother."*

We must work to rid our hearts of racial prejudice, socio-economic snobbery, and religious superiority. None of that belongs in the life of someone who wants to Live a love Life like Jesus loves.

3. THE LOVE LIFE HATES SIN

We must not equate love with complete acceptance of everything someone does. Jesus did not tolerate sin, deception, or false followers. He was painfully direct with the Pharisees, religious leaders, and those who claimed to love Him but loved their lives more. While still loving them, Jesus rebuked the Pharisees, calling them "Hypocrites!" and "Blind fools!" (Matthew 23:13, 16).

Matthew 23:13—*"But woe to you, scribes and Pharisees, hypocrites! For you shut the kingdom of heaven in people's faces. For you neither enter yourselves nor allow those who would enter to go in."*

Matthew 23:16—*"Woe to you, blind guides, who say, 'If anyone swears by the temple, it is nothing, but if anyone swears by the gold of the temple, he is bound by his oath.'*

He challenged the religious leaders with the warning, *"Not all who say to me, 'Lord, Lord' will enter the kingdom of heaven. Only the one who does the will of my Father in heaven"* (Matthew 7:21).

He baffled the half-hearted by telling them, *"No one who puts a hand to the plow and looks back is fit for the kingdom of heaven"* (Luke 9:62).

4. THE LOVE LIFE SHARES THE GOSPEL BOLDLY IN LOVE

Loving like Jesus means we care enough about the souls of others to tell them the truth in love. A rich young ruler came to Jesus with good intentions, but with a lack of surrender (Luke 18:18–25).

Luke 18:18–25 (ESV): *"And a ruler asked him, "Good Teacher, what must I do to inherit eternal life?" 19 And Jesus said to him, "Why do you call me good? No one is good except God alone. 20 You know the commandments: 'Do not commit adultery, Do not murder, Do not steal, Do not bear false witness, Honor your father and mother.'" 21 And he said, "All these I have kept from my youth." 22 When Jesus heard this, he said to him, "One thing you still lack. Sell all that you have and distribute to the poor, and you will have treasure in heaven; and come, follow me." 23 But when he heard these things, he became very sad, for he was extremely rich. 24 Jesus, seeing that he had become sad, said, "How difficult it is for those who have wealth to enter the kingdom of God! 25 For it is easier for a camel to go through the eye of a needle than for a rich person to enter the kingdom of God."*

He wanted what Jesus offered, but he did not want Jesus. He loved his money more, and Jesus lovingly pointed out the young man's greed. We do not love people by watering down the gospel that could save them. Jesus never changed the truth to satisfy the "itching ears" of His listeners (2 Timothy 4:3).

2 Timothy 4:3—*"For the time is coming when people will not endure sound teaching, but having itching ears they will accumulate for themselves teachers to suit their own passions,*

He loved them enough to warn them, challenge them, teach them, and forgive them all the way to the cross.

Luke 23:34— *"And Jesus said, "Father, forgive them, for they know not what they do." And they cast lots to divide his garments."*

5. THE LOVE LIFE FORGIVES

Forgiveness is another way we can Live a love life like Jesus. We forgive when we have been wronged (Matthew 6:14; Ephesians 4:32).

"For if you forgive others their trespasses, your heavenly Father will also forgive you,"

"Be kind to one another, tender-hearted, forgiving one another, as God in Christ forgave you."

Our selfishness wants to hang on to the wound, cherishing it, cradling it, and reliving it. But Jesus forgave and tells us to forgive as well (Mark 11:25).

"And whenever you stand praying, forgive, if you have anything against anyone, so that your Father also who is in heaven may forgive you your trespasses."

We cannot love someone we will not forgive. Jesus does not hold our forgiven sins over us; rather, He pronounces us clean and restored (1 John 1:9).

"If we confess our sins, he is faithful and just to forgive us our sins and to cleanse us from all unrighteousness."

There may be consequences for our sin, but He loves us through them and helps us learn from them. When we forgive someone, we can love and pray for that person with a clean conscience because we have done what God commands us to do (Colossians 3:13; Ephesians 4:32).

"Bearing with one another and, if one has a complaint against another, forgiving each other; as the Lord has forgiven you, so you also must forgive."

"Be kind to one another, tender-hearted, forgiving one another, as God in Christ forgave you."

Jesus told His disciples that the primary way the world would know they were His was by their love for one another (John 13:35).

"By this all people will know that you are my disciples, if you have love for one another."

If we love Jesus, then we will love what He loves, which is people. And as we practice loving like He loved, we become more like Him.

CONCLUSION

The Love Life is generous, without prejudice and favouritism, hates sin but love sinners, shares the gospel boldly in love, and forgives unconditionally in love.

2

THE LORD LOVES PEOPLE (PART 1)

30 And you shall love the Lord your God with all your heart, with all your soul, with all your mind, and with all your strength.' This is the first commandment. 31 And the second, like it, is this: 'You shall love your neighbor as yourself.' There is no other commandment greater than these. "—Mark 12:30-31

PURPOSE

To understand the Lord as the Lord of Love, and to know that the Lord of Love, loves you more than you know and think.

LUKE 8:1-15

After this, Jesus traveled about from one town and village to another, proclaiming the good news of the kingdom of God. The Twelve were with him, 2 and also some women who had been cured of evil spirits and diseases: Mary (called Magdalene) from whom seven demons had come out; 3 Joanna the wife of Chuza, the manager of Herod's household; Susanna; and many others. These women were helping to support them out of their own means. 4 While a large crowd was gathering and people were coming to Jesus from town after town, he told this parable: 5 "A farmer went out to sow his seed. As he was scattering the seed, some fell along the path; it was trampled on, and the birds ate it up. *⁶Some fell on rocky ground, and when it came up, the plants withered because they had no moisture. ⁷Other seed fell among thorns, which grew up with it and choked the plants. ⁸Still other seed fell on good soil. It came up and yielded a crop, a hundred times more than was sown." When he said this, he called out, "Whoever has ears to hear, let them hear." ⁹His disciples asked him what this parable meant. ¹⁰He said, "The knowledge of the secrets of the kingdom of God has been given to you, but to others I speak in parables, so that, "'though seeing, they may not see; though hearing, they may not understand.' ¹¹"This is the meaning of the parable:* **The seed is the word of God**. *¹²Those along the path are the ones who hear, and then the devil comes and takes away the word from their hearts, so that they may not believe and be saved. ¹³Those on the rocky ground are the ones who receive the word with joy when they hear it, but they have no root. They believe for a while, but in the time of testing they fall away. ¹⁴The seed that fell among thorns stands for those who hear, but as they go on their way they are choked by life's worries, riches, and pleasures, and they do not mature. ¹⁵But the seed on good soil stands for those with a noble and good heart, who hear the word, retain it, and by persevering produce a crop.*

6.   THE LORD LOVES THE MARGINALIZED

After this, **Jesus** *traveled about from one* **town** *and* **village** *to another,* **proclaiming the good news of the kingdom of God.** *The Twelve were with him, ²and also some women who had been cured of evil spirits and diseases:* **Mary** *(called Magdalene) from whom seven demons had come out; ³***Joanna** *the wife of* **Chuza,** *the manager of Herod's household;* **Susanna;** *and many others.* **These women** *were helping to support them out of their own means. ⁴ While a large crowd was gathering, and people were coming to Jesus from town after town.*

- The towners.
- The villages.
- The twelve
- The women
- The large Crowd

Note: The men spread the message outside the community, and the women strengthened the community from within by their "service." The individual names show that the question of authority was solved by *personal* responsibility. The women's service had its roots in miraculous healings, whereas the men's preaching was legitimated by their calling.[2]

Jesus loves all and accept all in His service.

Who do you love? What kind of people do you like, engage, relate with, serve, and love?

7. THE LORD LOVES PEOPLE OF ALL HEARTS

*⁴ While a large crowd was gathering and people were coming to Jesus from town after town, he told this **parable:** ⁵ "A **farmer** went out to*

---

[2] Bovon, F., & Koester, H. (2002). *Luke 1: a commentary on the Gospel of Luke 1:1–9:50* (pp. 299–300). Minneapolis, MN: Fortress Press.

*sow his seed. As he was **scattering the seed**, some fell along **the path**; it was trampled on, and the birds ate it up. ⁶ Some fell on **rocky ground**, and when it came up, the plants withered because they had no moisture. ⁷ Other seed fell among **thorns,** which grew up with it and choked the plants. ⁸ Still other seed fell on **good soil**. It came up and yielded a crop, a hundred times more than was sown."*

a. What is the parable saying?

People display different hearts:

- Road Ground
- Rocky Ground
- Thorny Ground
- Good Ground

Note: The Lord desires all hearts to hear Him. When He said this, He called out, *"**Whoever has ears to hear, let them hear.**"*

b. What does the parable mean?

The Lord explains things to His disciples.

*⁹ His disciples asked him what this parable meant. ¹⁰ He said, "The knowledge of the secrets of the kingdom of God has been given to you, but to others **I speak in parables**, so that, "'though seeing, they may not see; though hearing, they may not understand.' ¹¹ "This is the meaning of the parable: **The seed is the word of God**. ¹² Those **along the path are the ones who hear, and then the devil comes*** *and takes away the word from their hearts, so that they may not believe and be saved. [13] Those on the rocky ground are the ones who receive the word with joy when they hear it, but they have no root. They believe for a while, but in the time of testing they fall away. [14] The seed that fell among thorns stands for those who hear, but as they go on their way they are choked by life's worries, riches, and pleasures, and they do not mature. [15] But the seed on good soil stands for those with a noble and good heart, who hear the word, retain it, and by persevering produce a crop.*

- The Seed—The Word of God.
- The Road ground
- The Rocky ground
- The Thorny ground
- The Good ground

The Lord Loves all people and wants them saved. Salvation comes through Him alone, **who is the Word**, through the Preaching of the Good News of the Kingdom.

CONCLUSION

The Lord is Love. His love is to those who are least loved, the difficult to love and the loveable. No matter your heart type you can trust Him to love you unconditionally.

Small Group Lesson: THE LORD LOVES PEOPLE

And you shall love the LORD your God with all your heart, with all your soul, with all your mind, and with all your strength. This is the first commandment. And the second, like it, is this: 'You shall love your neighbor as yourself.' There is no other commandment greater than these. **~Mark 12:30-31**

INTRODUCTION – Though we are incomplete, God loves us completely. Though we are imperfect, He loves us perfectly. Though we may feel lost and without compass, God's love encompasses us completely. He loves every one of us, even those who are flawed, rejected, marginalized, awkward, sorrowful, or broken.

TALK IT OVER

You are not what others think you are. You are what God says you are.

1. **THE LORD LOVES THE MARGINALIZED**
   Society accepts & hails the wealthy, gifted and prominent but...

   - **God does not show PARTIALITY**
     For God shows no partiality [no arbitrary favoritism; with Him one person is not more important than another]. **~Rom 2:11**

- **God Loves & Accepts the POOR & HOMESLESS**
  The Spirit of the Lord is on me, because he has anointed me
  > to proclaim good news to the poor.   *~ Luke 4:18*

- **God Loves all races, and the outcast in society**
  The Lord builds up Jerusalem; He gathers the outcasts of Israel.   **~ Psalm 142:2**

2. THE LORD LOVES PEOPLE OF ALL HEARTS
- **The UNBELIEVING Heart**
  But God demonstrates his own love for us in this: While we were still sinners, Christ died for us.   ~
  Rom 3:8

- **The HARD Hearted**
  A new heart also will I give you, and a new spirit will I put within you: and I will take away the stony heart out of your flesh, and I will give you an heart of flesh.
  ~ **Ezek 36:26**

- **The BROKEN and a CONTRITE Heart**
  My [only] sacrifice [acceptable] to God is a broken spirit; A broken and contrite heart [broken with sorrow for sin, thoroughly penitent], such, O God, You will not despise.
  ~Psalm 51:17

- **The PURE in Heart**

God blesses those whose hearts are pure, for they will see God.   ~ **Matt 5:8**

DISCOVERY QUESTIONS

1. How can we show love to All People?

2. Who is the kind of people you like to, engage, relate with, and love?

PRAYER DIRECTION

1. Dear God, teach and help me to love All People like you do.

2. Lord Jesus, help me to love people for who they are and not what they have or done. Amen

3

THE LORD LOVES PEOPLE (PART 2)

¹⁹ Then his mother and his brothers came to him, but they could not reach him because of the crowd. ²⁰ And he was told, "Your mother and your brothers are standing outside, desiring to see you." ²¹ But he answered them, "My mother and my brothers are those who hear the word of God and do it."—Luke 8:19-21

PURPOSE

To understand that the Lord is love. His love is seen in how He overcame nature, exorcised demons, healed from diseases, and raised people from death to show that He could overcome every type of enemy that opposes humankind.

Last lesson, we learnt that the Lord is Love—He loves:

- The towners
- The villagers
- The women
- The disciples
- The hearts

TEXT:
LUKE 8:22-25

1. The Lord Calms the Storm

[22] One day he got into a boat with his disciples, and he said to them, "Let us go across to the other side of the lake." So, they set out, [23] and as they sailed, he fell asleep. And a windstorm came down on the lake, and they were filling with water and were in danger. [24] And they went and woke him, saying, "Master, Master, we are perishing!" And he awoke and rebuked the wind and the raging waves, and they ceased, and there was a calm. [25] He said to them, "Where is your faith?" And they were afraid, and they marveled, saying to one another, "Who then is this, that he commands even winds and water, and they obey him?"

The point of the story is not simply that Jesus could still the storm, but rather that the disciples should have trusted His power to help them.[3]

WHEN PEACE LIKE A RIVER[4]

Horatio G. Spafford was a successful lawyer and businessman in Chicago with a lovely family—a wife, Anna, and five children. However, they were not strangers to tears and tragedy. Their young son died with pneumonia in 1871, and in that same year, much of their business was lost in the great Chicago fire. Yet, God

---

[3] Marshall, I. H. (1978). *The Gospel of Luke: a commentary on the Greek text* (p. 334). Exeter: Paternoster Press.

[4] Story behind the song: It is well with my soul.
https://www.staugustine.com/article/20141016/LIFESTYLE/310169936

in His mercy and kindness allowed the business to flourish once more.

On Nov. 21, 1873, the French ocean liner, Ville du Havre was crossing the Atlantic from the U.S. to Europe with 313 passengers on board. Among the passengers were Mrs. Spafford and their four daughters. Although Mr. Spafford had planned to go with his family, he found it necessary to stay in Chicago to help solve an unexpected business problem. He told his wife he would join her and their children in Europe a few days later. His plan was to take another ship.

About four days into the crossing of the Atlantic, the Ville du Harve collided with a powerful, iron-hulled Scottish ship, the Loch Earn. Suddenly, all of those on board were in grave danger. Anna hurriedly brought her four children to the deck. She knelt there with Annie, Margaret Lee, Bessie and Tanetta and prayed that God would spare them if that could be His will, or to make them willing to endure whatever awaited them. Within approximately 12 minutes, the Ville du Harve slipped beneath the dark waters of the Atlantic, carrying with it 226 of the passengers including the four Spafford children.

A sailor, rowing a small boat over the spot where the ship went down, spotted a woman floating on a piece of the wreckage. It was Anna, still alive. He pulled her into the boat and they were picked up by another large vessel which, nine days later, landed them in Cardiff, Wales. From there she wired her husband a message which began, "Saved alone, what shall I do?" Mr. Spafford later framed the telegram and placed it in his office.

Another of the ship's survivors, Pastor Weiss, later recalled Anna saying, "God gave me four daughters. Now they have been taken from me. Someday I will understand why."

Mr. Spafford booked passage on the next available ship and left to join his grieving wife. With the ship about four days out, the captain called Spafford to his cabin and told him they were over the place where his children went down.

According to Bertha Spafford Vester, a daughter born after the tragedy, Spafford wrote *"It Is Well With My Soul"* while on this journey.

> *When peace like a river attendeth my way,*
> *When sorrows like sea billows roll,*
> *Whatever my lot, Thou hast taught me to say,*
> *It is well, it is well with my soul.*
>
> **Chorus:**
> *It is well with my soul,*
> *It is well, it is well with my soul*

- The Lord loves people in all life circumstances.
- The Lord expects people going through storms to turn to Him.

- The Lord desires His lovers and followers to learn to trust Him in their time of storm.
- The Lord want us to be storm-stoppers. Whose storm can you help calm in love?
- How willing are you to trust the Lord to see you through the storm?

2. The Lord Heals Demon-possessed Man.

26 Then they sailed to the country of the Gerasenes, which is opposite Galilee. 27 When Jesus had stepped out on land, there met him a man from the city who had demons. For a long time, he had worn no clothes, and he had not lived in a house but among the tombs. 28 When he saw Jesus, he cried out and fell down before him and said with a loud voice, "What have you to do with me, Jesus, Son of the Most High God? I beg you, do not torment me." 29 For he had commanded the unclean spirit to come out of the man. (For many a time it had seized him. He was kept under guard and bound with chains and shackles, but he would break the bonds and be driven by the demon into the desert.) 30 Jesus then asked him, "What is your name?" And he said, "Legion," for many demons had entered him. 31 And they begged him not to command them to depart into the abyss. 32 Now a large herd of pigs was feeding there on the hillside, and they begged him to let them enter these. So, he gave them permission. 33 Then the demons came out of the man and entered the pigs, and the herd rushed down the steep bank into the lake and drowned. 34 When the herdsmen saw what had happened, they fled and told it in the city and in the country. 35 Then people went out to see what had happened, and they came to Jesus and found the man from whom the demons had gone, sitting at the feet of Jesus, clothed and in his right mind, and they were afraid. ³⁶ And those who had seen it told them how the demon-possessed man had been healed. ³⁷ Then all the people of the surrounding country of the Gerasenes asked him to depart from them, for they were seized with great fear. So, he got into the boat and returned. ³⁸ The man from whom the demons had gone begged that he might be with him, but Jesus sent him away, saying, ³⁹ "Return to your home, and declare how much God has done for you." And he went away, proclaiming throughout the whole city how much Jesus had done for him.

The main point is the demonstration of the power of Jesus to deal with an especially severe case of demon possession; through Jesus God did great things for an unhappy victim (8:39)[5]

- The Lord loves the demon-possessed.
- The Lord has power over demonic forces and powers—trust in Him.
- The Lord wants us to know and take spiritual forces seriously because it is real.
- Which demon-possessed person can you cast out in love this week?
- The Lord delivers you, so you can share Him with your people first.

---

[5] Marshall, I. H. (1978). *The Gospel of Luke: a commentary on the Greek text* (p. 335). Exeter: Paternoster Press.

3. The Lord Heals a Woman with the Issue of Blood

As Jesus went, the people pressed around him. [43] And there was a woman who had had a discharge of blood for twelve years, and though she had spent all her living on physicians,[f] she could not be healed by anyone. [44] She came up behind him and touched the fringe of his garment, and immediately her discharge of blood ceased. [45] And Jesus said, "Who was it that touched me?" When all denied it, Peter said, "Master, the crowds surround you and are pressing in on you!" [46] But Jesus said, "Someone touched me, for I perceive that power has gone out from me." [47] And when the woman saw that she was not hidden, she came trembling, and falling down before him declared in the presence of all the people why she had touched him, and how she had been immediately healed. [48] And he said to her, "Daughter, your faith has made you well; go in peace."

This pair of stories demonstrate the power of Jesus over disease and death[6]

- A timid faith can become a testifying faith-How willing are you to share how He has been goo to you with others.
- Faith in this sense is in full speed ahead.

---

[6] Marshall, I. H. (1978). *The Gospel of Luke: a commentary on the Greek text* (p. 341). Exeter: Paternoster Press.

4. The Lord Raises Jairus's Daughter.

⁴⁰ Now when Jesus returned, the crowd welcomed him, for they were all waiting for him. ⁴¹ And there came a man named Jairus, who was a ruler of the synagogue. And falling at Jesus' feet, he implored him to come to his house, ⁴² for he had an only daughter, about twelve years of age, and she was dying. ⁴⁹ While he was still speaking, someone from the ruler's house came and said, "Your daughter is dead; do not trouble the Teacher any more." ⁵⁰ But Jesus on hearing this answered him, "Do not fear; only believe, and she will be well." ⁵¹ And when he came to the house, he allowed no one to enter with him, except Peter and John and James, and the father and mother of the child. ⁵² And all were weeping and mourning for her, but he said, "Do not weep, for she is not dead but sleeping." ⁵³ And they laughed at him, knowing that she was dead. ⁵⁴ But taking her by the hand he called, saying, "Child, arise." ⁵⁵ And her spirit returned, and she got up at once. And he directed that something should be given her to eat. ⁵⁶ And her parents were amazed, but he charged them to tell no one what had happened.

- The Lord loves women and little girls as they are.
- Who is the woman or the girl in your life who needs your love?
- Trusting in the Lord's love and care means accepting His timing for events.
- Faith must be patient and wait on the Lord's timing.

Family and friends

- Our lives require a vibrant faith applied to the affairs of life, but it also requires a patient waiting on the Lord, for the Father does know best.
- What God the Father did in the Old Testament, Jesus the Son did in the New Testament, God the Holy Spirit is doing in us and through us in Jesus' name.

CONCLUSION

The Lord of Love loves us. He has power over the elements, the demonic world, diseases, and death. He is the Lord of Love and deals with us according to His unfailing love.

4

THE LORD IS LOVE (PART 3)—LOVE MADE HIM RIDE

⁹Rejoice greatly, Daughter Zion! Shout, Daughter Jerusalem! See, your king comes to you, righteous and victorious, lowly, and riding on a donkey, on a colt, the foal of a donkey.—Zech. 9:9

SCRIPTURES:

Matthew 21:1-11; Mark 11:1-10; Luke 19:28-44; John 12:12-19

PURPOSE:

To encourage us to not take the unfailing, faithful, and sacrificial love of our Lord for granted.

THE TEXT:

*As they approached Jerusalem and came to Bethphage on the Mount of Olives, Jesus sent two disciples, ² saying to them, "Go to the village ahead of you, and at once you will find a donkey tied there, with her colt by her. Untie them and bring them to me. ³ If anyone says anything to you, say that the **Lord needs them**, and he will send them right away." ⁴ This took place to fulfill what was spoken through* *the prophet:* ^{5} *"Say to Daughter Zion, 'See, your king comes to you, gentle and riding on a donkey, and on a colt, the foal of a donkey.'"* ^{6} *The disciples went and did as Jesus had instructed them.* ^{7} *They brought the donkey and the colt and placed their cloaks on them for Jesus to sit on.* ^{8} *A very large crowd spread their cloaks on the road, while others cut branches from the trees and spread them on the road.* ^{9} *The crowds that went ahead of him and those that followed shouted, "Hosanna to the Son of David!" "Blessed is he who comes in the name of the Lord!" "Hosanna in the highest heaven!"*

Psalm 118:25,26

^{25}*LORD, save us! LORD, grant us success!* ^{26}*Blessed is he who comes in the name of the LORD. From the house of the LORD, we bless you.*

Questions for the Day

1. Why did Jesus go to Jerusalem at this time?
2. Why did Jesus make the decision to ride on a donkey?
3. Did Jesus know what was going to happen to him in Jerusalem?
4. Why did Jesus choose to go knowing what awaited him?

OFFICER ERIC TALLEY, FATHER AND 'DEVOUT CHRISTIAN,' ONE OF 10 KILLED IN BOULDER SHOOTING[7]

Officer Eric Talley was one of 10 people killed in a mass shooting Monday in Boulder, Colorado. Talley was a husband, a father of seven, and a devoted follower of Jesus.

Officer Eric Talley was the first to arrive at the scene, said Herold, who described his actions as "nothing short of heroic." Boulder County District Attorney Michael Dougherty said, *"He died charging into the line of fire trying to save people who were simply trying to live their lives and go food shopping."*

This is what I think about Officer Eric Talley: His love for God, country and his citizens.

William Rainey once said, " *Why didn't somebody ever tell me that I could become a Christian and work on all my doubt afterward?"* The fact is every little step you take toward Christ moves you further away from the Six "D"s —**doubt, discouragement, depression, demonization, disease, and despair.**

We are all moving, but sometimes we move slowly. Are *you struggling with one of these "D" issues?*

---

[7] https://churchleaders.com/news/393022-eric-talley-christian-shooting.html

Are you **doubting God's love** because you are in a crisis? "God! I have just found out I have a terminal illness! Don't you love me?"

Are you **discouraged because you do not think he cares** for you? "God! Don't you see the trouble I am in? Don't you care?"

Are you **depressed because life has not turned out the way you thought** it would? "God! My spouse is leaving me! Can't you stop this from happening?"

Are you wondering whether your **situation is demonic or not?** "God, I do not understand what am going through—is it Satan and his cohort?"

Are you battling one **disease or another and do not seem to know when your healing** will become a reality? "Lord, my health; I need your healing."

Are you **despairing because you do not think he is forgiven you for your latest sin?** "God! I still feel guilty. Haven't you forgiven me?"

The Bible makes this statement in 1 John 5:13: *"These things I have written to you who believe in the name of the Son of God, so that you may know that you have eternal life"* (NASB).

There is a lot we do not know, but the most important question has already been answered.

The things written in God's Word are written so that **you may know absolutely, for sure, for certain, and with confidence that when you die you are going to Heaven.**

Let us try to find some answers from the ride Jesus took.

1. WHY DID JESUS GO TO JERUSALEM AT THIS TIME?

*As they approached Jerusalem and came to Bethphage on the Mount of Olives, Jesus sent two disciples, ² saying to them, "Go to the village ahead of you, and at once you will find a donkey tied there, with her colt by her. Untie them and bring them to me. ³ If anyone says anything to you, say that the **Lord needs them**, and he will send them right away."*

a. **His time was drawing near.**
   John 12: 27—*Now my soul is deeply troubled. Should I pray, 'Father, save me from this hour'? But this is the very reason I came!*

b. His Fathers will for the world, demanded it.

c. His arrest, trial, maltreatment, crucifixion, death, resurrection, and ascension must take place in Jerusalem.

d. His love for the Father and sinful humanity compelled Him.

e. His way of showing His disciples the kingdom way
John 12:15—*Anyone who loves their life will lose it, while anyone who hates their life in this world will keep it for eternal life.*

2. WHY DID JESUS MAKE THE DECISION TO RIDE ON A DONKEY?

a. To fulfill the Messianic prophecy

⁴ This took place to fulfill what was spoken through the prophet: ⁵ "Say to Daughter Zion, 'See, your king comes to you, gentle and riding on a donkey, and on a colt, the foal of a donkey.'"

Look at how John the beloved put's it:

"Don't be afraid, people of Jerusalem. Look, your King is coming, riding on a donkey's colt." ¹⁶ His disciples did not understand at the time that this was a fulfillment of prophecy. But after Jesus entered into his glory, they remembered what had happened and realized that these things had been written about him.

b. To reveal Himself as a humble King.

He was solemnly entering as a humble King of peace. Traditionally, entering the city on a **donkey** symbolizes arrival in peace, rather than as a war-waging king arriving on a horse.

c. To reveal the Savior.

[11] The LORD has made proclamation to the ends of the earth: "Say to Daughter Zion, 'See, your Savior comes! See, his reward is with him, and his recompense accompanies him.'"—Isaiah 62:11

[25]LORD, save us! LORD, grant us success! [26]Blessed is he who comes in the name of the LORD. From the house of the LORD, we bless you.—Psalm 118:25,26

3. DID JESUS KNOW WHAT WAS GOING TO HAPPEN TO HIM JERUSALEM?

a. Yes, but how did we know that? He told his disciples.

[32] They were on their way up to Jerusalem, with Jesus leading the way, and the disciples were astonished, while those who followed were afraid. Again, he took the Twelve aside and told them what was going to happen to him. [33] "We are going up to Jerusalem," he said, "and the Son of Man will be delivered over to the chief priests and the teachers of the law. They will condemn him to death and will hand him over to the Gentiles, [34] who will mock him and spit on him, flog him and kill him. Three days later he will rise."—Mark 10:32-34 NIV.

4. WHY DID JESUS CHOOSE TO GO KNOWING WHAT AWAITS HIM?

a. **To accomplish the purpose for which He came to the earth.** To restore sinners to their God so that they may have eternal life forever with him.

For God so loved the world that he gave his one and only Son, that whoever believes in him shall not perish but have eternal life. (**John 3:16**)

b. **To be obedient to the Father's will.**
Father, if you are willing, please take this cup of suffering away from me. Yet I want your will to be done, not mine." (**Luke 22:42**)

c. **To reveal his willingness to sacrifice his life.**

No one can take my life from me. I sacrifice it voluntarily. For I have the authority to lay it down when I want to and also to take it up again. For this is what my Father has commanded." (John 10:18)

d. **To show His love for humanity. (John 3:16)**
His love compelled him to go to Jerusalem as part of the redemptive plan.
[10] For the Son of Man came to seek and to save the lost." Luke 19:10.

e. **To show us what will happen in eternity.**

[9] After this I looked, and behold, a great multitude that no one could number, from every nation, from all tribes and peoples

and languages, standing before the throne and before the Lamb, clothed in white robes, with palm branches in their hands, [10] and crying out with a loud voice, "Salvation belongs to our God who sits on the throne, and to the Lamb!" [11] And all the angels were standing around the throne and around the elders and the four living creatures, and they fell on their faces before the throne and worshiped God, [12] saying, "Amen! Blessing and glory and wisdom and thanksgiving and honor and power and might be to our God forever and ever! Amen." Revelation 7:9-12. (ESV)

CONCLUSION

For Jesus, His love for God and for sinful humanity made Him ride a donkey. How about you?

5

CHRIST THE ULTIMATE LOVE (PART 1): "LOVE TOOK HIM TO GETHSEMANE"

² And if I have prophetic powers, and understand all mysteries and all knowledge, and if I have all faith, so as to remove mountains, but have not love, I am nothing. 3 If I give away all I have, and if I deliver up my body to be burned, but have not love, I gain nothing.— 1 Corinthians 13:2-3

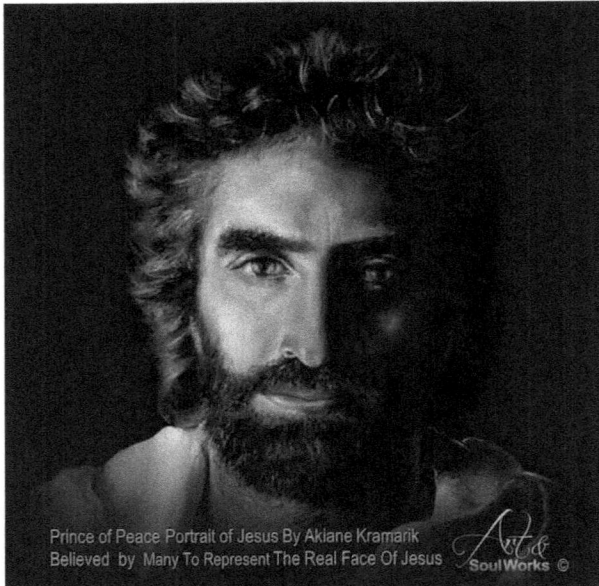

Prince of Peace Portrait of Jesus By Akiane Kramarik
Believed by Many To Represent The Real Face Of Jesus

The face of Jesus: what do you see?

THE TEXT:

Matthew 26:36-46. Mark 14:32-42; Luke 22:39-46

*36 Then Jesus went with them to a place called Gethsemane, and he said to his disciples, "Sit here, **while I go over there and pray.**" 37 And taking with him **Peter** and the **two sons of Zebedee,** he began to be **sorrowful and troubled.** 38 Then he said to them, "**My soul is very sorrowful, even to death; remain here, and watch**[a] **with me.**" 39 And going a little farther he fell on his face and prayed, saying, "My Father, if it be possible, let this cup pass from me; nevertheless, **not as I will, but as you will.**" 40 And he came to the disciples and found them sleeping. And he said to Peter, "So, could you not watch with **me one hour?** 41 **Watch and pray that you may not enter into temptation. The spirit indeed is willing, but the flesh is weak.**" 42 Again, for the second time, he went away and prayed, "My Father, if this cannot pass unless I drink it, **your will be done.**" 43 And again he came and found them sleeping, for their eyes were heavy. 44 So, leaving them again, **he went away and prayed for the third time, saying the same words again.** 45 Then he came to the disciples and said to them, "Sleep and take your rest later on.*[b]* *See,* **the hour is at hand,** *and the* **Son of Man is betrayed** *into the hands of sinners.* 46 **Rise,** *let us be going; see,* **my betrayer is at hand.**"*— MATTHEW 26:36-46

*39 **And He came out and went, as was His habit, to the Mount of Olives;** and the disciples also followed Him. 40 Now when He arrived at the place, He said to them, "**Pray that you do not come*** *into temptation.*" *⁴¹ And He withdrew from them about a stone's throw, and He knelt* **down and began to pray,** *⁴² saying,* **"Father, if You are willing, remove this cup from Me; yet not My will, but Yours be done.**" *⁴³ [[a]* **Now an angel from heaven appeared to Him, strengthening Him.** *⁴⁴* **And being in agony, He was praying very fervently; and His sweat became like drops of blood, falling down upon the ground].** *⁴⁵ When He rose from prayer, He came to the disciples and found them sleeping from sorrow, ⁴⁶ and He said to them, "Why are you sleeping? Get up and pray that you do not come into temptation.*"—Luke 22:39-46

³² They came to a place named Gethsemane; and **He said to His disciples,** *"Sit here until I* **have prayed.**" *³³ And He* **took with Him Peter, James, and John, and began to be very distressed and troubled.** *³⁴ And He said to them,* **"My soul is deeply grieved, to the point of death; remain here and keep watch.**" *³⁵ And He went a little beyond them, and fell to the ground and began praying that if it were possible, the hour might pass Him by. ³⁶ And He was saying,* **"Abba! Father! All things are possible for You; remove this cup from Me; yet not what I will, but what You will.**" *³⁷ And He came and found them sleeping, and said to* **Peter,** *"*Simon, *are you asleep? Could you not keep watch for one hour? ³⁸Keep watching and praying, so that you will not come into temptation; the spirit is willing, but the flesh is weak.*" *³⁹ And again He went away and prayed, saying the same words. ⁴⁰ And again He came and found them sleeping, for their eyes were heavy; and they did not know what to say in reply to Him. ⁴¹ And He came the third time, and said to them, "Are you still sleeping and resting? That is enough. The hour has come; behold,* **the Son of Man is being betrayed into the hands of** *sinners.* ⁴² ***Get up, let us go;*** *behold, the one who is betraying Me is near!"*—Mark 14:32-42.

DEFINITION

Ultimate: "the best achievable or imaginable of its kind" the best or most extreme of its kind.

SYNONYMS. best, ideal, greatest, supreme, paramount, superlative, highest, unsurpassed, unrivalled, topmost, utmost, optimum, quintessential.

The Garden of Gethsemane 2017

1- Mama Olivia

QUESTIONS

A. HOW DID JESUS DEAL WITH HIS GETHSEMANE?

1. JESUS FACED IT WITH FAITH AND LOVE.

> *[36] Then Jesus went with them to a place called Gethsemane, [39] And He came out and went, as was His habit, to the Mount of Olives. and the disciples also followed Him. [32] They came to a place named Gethsemane.*

How do you face your Gethsemane?

2. JESUS ASKED FOR PRAY.

> *and he said to his disciples, "Sit here, **while I go over there and pray." [40] Now when He arrived at the place, He said to them, "Pray that you do not come into temptation."***

> *[40] And he came to the disciples and found them sleeping. And he said to Peter, "So, could you not watch with **me one hour? He said to His disciples, "Sit here until I have prayed." [34] And He said to them, "My soul is deeply grieved, to the point of death; remain here and keep watch."***

> *[41] And He came the third time, and said to them, "Are you still sleeping and resting?*

Who do you have praying with you and for you?

3. JESUS WENT FURTHER WITH HIS INNER CIRCLE.

*37 And taking with him **Peter** and the **two sons of Zebedee**, he began to be **sorrowful and troubled**. 38 Then he said to them, "**My soul is very sorrowful, even to death**. Again, for the second time, he went away and prayed, "My Father, if this cannot pass unless I drink it, **your will be done**." So, leaving them again, **he went away and prayed for the third time, saying the same words again**. 41 And He withdrew from them about a stone's throw, and He knelt **down and began to pray**, 42 saying, "**Father, if You are willing, remove this cup from Me; yet not My will, but Yours be done**."*

*33 And He **took with Him Peter, James, and John, and began to be very distressed and troubled** 39 And again He went away and prayed, saying the same words. 40 And again He came and found them sleeping, for their eyes were heavy; and they did not know what to say in reply to Him.*

Who is in your inner circle? Who is your prayer mate?

4. JESUS SHARED HIS FEELING WITH HIS CLOSE FRIENDS.

*37 And taking with him **Peter** and the **two sons of Zebedee**, he began to be **sorrowful and troubled**. 38 Then he said to them, "**My soul is very sorrowful, even to death; remain here, and watch with me**."*

*37 And He came and *found them sleeping, and said to **Peter**, "**Simon**, are you asleep? Could you not keep watch for one* *hour? ³⁸ Keep watching and praying, so that you will not come into temptation; the spirit is willing, but the flesh is weak."*

Who do you share your deep emotions with? Who are you vulnerable with?

5. JESUS ASKED THEM TO WATCH WITH HIM.

*⁴⁰ Now when He arrived at the place, He said to them, "**Pray that you do not come into temptation." remain here, and watch with me.***"

Who is watching with you?

6. JESUS FELL ON HIS FACE AND PRAYED ON THREE OCCASIONS.

*³⁹ And going a little farther he fell on his face and prayed, saying, "My Father, if it be possible, let this cup pass from me; nevertheless, **not as I will, but as you will.**"*

Jesus rose and asked the disciples to arise and face the future with God.

*⁴³ **Now an angel from heaven appeared to Him, strengthening Him. ⁴⁴ And being in agony, He was praying very fervently; and His sweat became like drops of blood, falling down upon the ground**].*

³⁵ And He went a little beyond them, and fell to the ground and began praying that if it were possible, the hour might pass

*Him by. [36] And He was saying, "**Abba!** [e] **Father! All things are possible for You; remove this cup from Me; yet not what I will, but what You will.**"*

How intense, and how often do you pray?

7. JESUS ROSE AND ASKED HIS DISCIPLES TO ARISE

*[45] Then he came to the disciples and said to them, "Sleep and take your rest later on. See, **the hour is at hand**, and the **Son of Man is betrayed** into the hands of sinners. [46] **Rise,** let us be going; see, **my betrayer is at hand.**"*

[45] When He rose from prayer, He came to the disciples and found them sleeping from sorrow, [46] and He said to them, "Why are you sleeping? Get up and pray that you do not come into temptation."

*The hour has come; behold, **the Son of Man is being betrayed into the hands of sinners.** [42] **Get up, let us go;** behold, the one who is betraying Me is near.*

When do you know you have to rise up and move forward?

B. HOW SHOULD YOU DEAL WITH YOUR GETHSEMANE?

BE LIKE JESUS

- Love God and go in faith.
- Ask for prayers.
- Work with your inner circle
- Go further in prayer.
- Trust God for divine encounter and direction
- Live and do God's will.
- Rise and keep living.

CONCLUSION

- Prayer for salvation
- Prayer for rededication
- Prayer for the rest of the Easter and the month-Lord save souls this Easter and please use us.

6

CHRIST: THE ULTIMATE LOVE (PART 2): LOVE TOOK HIM THROUGH GRUESOME TREATMENT

KEY QUESTIONS

- How was Jesus treated? **GRUESOME**
- How did Jesus respond to the gruesome treatment?
- How do we respond to gruesome treatment as His followers?

SCRIPTURE:

Matthew 26:47-27:65

DEFINITION: *"Gruesome"*

Treatment causing repulsion or horror; grisly. Shocking. extremely unpleasant.

Synonyms:
grisly · ghastly · frightful · horrid · horrifying · fearful · hideous · macabre · spine-chilling · horrible · horrendous · grim · awful · dire · dreadful · terrible · horrific · disgusting

Synonyms:

unpleasant · disagreeable · disgusting · distasteful · awful · dreadful · horrible · terrible · vile · foul · abominable · frightful · loathsome · revolting · repulsive

BEFORE HIS ARREST, WE SEE:

- The plot against Jesus
- Jesus cleansing the temple.
- Jesus anointed at Bethany
- Jesus betrayed by Judas.
- Jesus at last Supper
- Jesus washes the feet of His disciples.
- Jesus prays for his disciples and for us.
- Jesus predicts Peter's denial
- Jesus at Gethsemane
- Jesus puts a cut ear back.

OUR PURPOSE:

Like Jesus, the world might treat us gruesomely but let us treat them with love and respect.

1. HOW WAS JESUS TREATED? GRUESOME

JESUS' ARREST

We will look at:

- Jesus Before the Sanhedrin,
- Jesus disowned by Peter,
- Jesus before Pilate,
- Jesus before the soldiers,
- Jesus crucified,
- Jesus dies,
- Jesus buried, and
- Jesus' tomb guarded.

⁴⁷ While he was still speaking, Judas, one of the Twelve, arrived. With him was a large crowd armed with swords and clubs, sent from the chief priests and the elders of the people. ⁴⁸ Now the betrayer had arranged a signal with them: **"The one I kiss is the man;** *arrest him."* ⁴⁹ *Going at once to Jesus, Judas said, "Greetings, Rabbi!" and kissed him. ⁵⁰ Jesus replied,* **"Do what you came for, friend."**

Question: Do you know how it feels like to be betrayed? By your trusted friend?

Then the men stepped forward, seized Jesus, and arrested him. ⁵¹ With that, one of Jesus' companions reached for his sword, drew it out and struck the servant of the high **priest, cutting off his ear.** ⁵² *"Put your sword back in its place," Jesus said to him, "for all who draw the sword will die by the sword. ⁵³ Do you think I cannot call on my Father, and he will at once put at my disposal more than twelve* legions of angels? *[54] But how then would the Scriptures be fulfilled that say it must happen in this way?"* *[55] In that hour Jesus said to the crowd, "Am I leading a rebellion, that you have come out with swords and clubs to capture me? Every day I sat in the temple courts teaching, and you did not arrest me.* *[56] But this has all taken place that the writings of the prophets might be fulfilled."* **Then all the disciples deserted him and fled.**

Question: How does it feel like to be deserted by your best of the best in your time of need?

1. Jesus Before the Sanhedrin.

[57] Those who had arrested Jesus took him to Caiaphas the high priest, where the teachers of the law and the elders had assembled. *[58] But Peter followed him at a distance, right up to the courtyard of the high priest. He entered and sat down with the guards to see the outcome.* *[59] The chief priests and the whole Sanhedrin were looking for false evidence against Jesus so that they could put him to death.* *[60] But they did not find any, though many false witnesses came forward. Finally, two came forward* *[61] and declared,* **"This fellow said, 'I am able to destroy the temple of God and rebuild it in three days.'"** *[62] Then the high priest stood up and said to Jesus, "Are you not going to answer? What is this testimony that these men are bringing against you?"* *[63]* **But Jesus remained silent.** *The high priest said to him, "I charge you under oath by the living God: Tell us if you are the Messiah, the Son of God."* *[64]* **"You have said so,"** *Jesus replied.* **"But I say to all of you: From now on you will see the Son of Man sitting at the right hand of the Mighty One and coming on**

the clouds of heaven." ⁶⁵ Then the high priest tore his clothes and said, "He has spoken blasphemy! Why do we need any more witnesses? Look, now you have heard the blasphemy. ⁶⁶ What do you think?" "He is worthy of death," they answered. ⁶⁷ Then they spit in his face and struck him with their fists. Others slapped him ⁶⁸ and said, "Prophesy to us, Messiah. Who hit you?"

Question: How does it feel like to be lied, spit, struck, slap, and be mocked?

2. Jesus disowned by Peter.

⁶⁹ Now Peter was sitting out in the courtyard, and a servant girl came to him. "You also were with Jesus of Galilee," she said. ⁷⁰ But he denied it before them all. "I don't know what you're talking about," he said. ⁷¹ Then he went out to the gateway, where another servant girl saw him and said to the people there, "This fellow was with Jesus of Nazareth." ⁷² He denied it again, with an oath: "I don't know the man!" ⁷³ After a little while, those standing there went up to Peter and said, "Surely you are one of them; your accent gives you away." ⁷⁴ Then he began to call down curses, and he swore to them, "I don't know the man!" Immediately a rooster crowed. ⁷⁵ Then Peter remembered the word Jesus had spoken: "Before the rooster crows, you will disown me three times." And he went outside and wept bitterly.

Question: How does it feel like to be disowned by someone you trusted and invested in all your life?

3. Jesus Before Pilate

¹¹ Meanwhile Jesus stood before the governor, and the governor asked him, "Are you the king of the Jews?" "You have said so," Jesus replied. ¹² When he was accused by the chief priests and the elders, he gave no answer. ¹³ Then Pilate asked him, "Don't you hear the testimony they are bringing against you?" ¹⁴ But Jesus made no reply, not even to a single charge—to the great amazement of the governor. ¹⁵ Now it was the governor's custom at the festival to release a prisoner chosen by the crowd. **¹⁶ At that time they had a well-known prisoner whose name was Jesus[b] Barabbas. ¹⁷ So when the crowd had gathered, Pilate asked them, "Which one do you want me to release to you: Jesus Barabbas, or Jesus who is called the Messiah?"** *¹⁸ For he knew it was out of self-interest that they had handed Jesus over to him. ¹⁹ While Pilate was sitting on the judge's seat,* **his wife** *sent him this message: "Don't have anything to do with that innocent man, for I have suffered a great deal today in a dream because of him." ²⁰ But the* **chief priests** *and* **the elders** *persuaded the crowd to ask for Barabbas and to have Jesus executed. ²¹ "Which of the two do you want me to release to you?" asked the governor. "Barabbas," they answered. ²² "What shall I do, then, with Jesus who is called the Messiah?" Pilate asked. They all answered,* **"Crucify him!"** *²³ "Why? What crime has he committed?" asked Pilate. But they shouted all the louder,* **"Crucify him!"** *²⁴ When Pilate saw that he was getting nowhere, but that instead an uproar was starting, he took water and washed his hands in front of the crowd. "I am innocent of this man's blood," he said. "It is your responsibility!"* **²⁵ All the people answered, "His blood is on us and on our children!"** *²⁶ Then he released Barabbas to them. But he had Jesus* **flogged,** *and handed him over* **to be crucified.**

Question: How does it feel like to see evil freed and the right disregarded?

4. Jesus mocked by the soldiers.

*[27] Then the governor's soldiers took Jesus into the Praetorium and gathered the whole company of soldiers around him. [28] They **stripped him** and **put a scarlet robe** on him, [29] and then **twisted together a crown of thorns and set it on his head**. They put a staff in his right hand. Then they **knelt in front of him and mocked him**. "Hail, king of the Jews!" they said. [30] They **spit on him and took the staff and struck him on the head again and again**. [31] After they had mocked him, they took off the robe and put his own clothes on him. Then they led him away to crucify him.*

Question: How does it feel like to be mocked by the people whose primary responsibility is to protect you?

5. Jesus crucified.

*[32] As they were going out, they met a man from Cyrene, named Simon, and they forced him to carry the cross. [33] They came to a place called Golgotha (which means "the place of the skull"). [34] There **they offered Jesus' wine to drink, mixed with gall; but after tasting it, he refused to drink it**. [35] When they had crucified him, they divided up his clothes by casting lots. [36] And sitting down, they kept watch over him there. [37] Above his head they placed the written charge against him: THIS IS JESUS, THE KING OF THE JEWS. [38] Two rebels were crucified with him, one on his right and one on his left. [39] Those*

who passed by **hurled insults at him,** *shaking their heads* [40] *and saying, "You who are going to destroy the temple and build it in three days, save yourself! Come down from the cross, if you are the Son of God!"* [41] **In the same way the chief priests, the teachers of the law and the elders mocked him.** [42] *"He saved others," they said, "but he can't save himself! He is the king of Israel! Let him come down now from the cross, and we will believe in him.* [43] *He trusts in God. Let God rescue him now if he wants him, for he said, 'I am the Son of God.'"* [44] *In the same way the rebels who were crucified with him also* **heaped insults on** *him.*

QUESTION: How does it feel like to be insulted by strangers, rebels, the Chief Priest and elders?

6. Jesus dies.

[45] *From noon until three in the afternoon darkness came over all the land.* [46] *About three in the afternoon* **Jesus cried out in a loud voice, "Eli, Eli, lema sabachthani?" (which means "My God, my God, why have you forsaken me?").** [47] *When some of those standing there heard this, they said, "He's calling Elijah."* [48] *Immediately one of them ran and got a sponge. He filled it with wine vinegar, put it on a staff, and offered it to Jesus to drink.* [49] *The rest said, "Now leave him alone. Let us see if Elijah comes to save him."*

Question: How does it feel like to be rejected or forsaken by your Father?

7. Jesus Buried

*⁵⁷ As evening approached, there **came a rich man from Arimathea**, named Joseph, who had himself become a disciple of Jesus. ⁵⁸ Going to Pilate, he asked for Jesus' body, and Pilate ordered that it be given to him. ⁵⁹ Joseph took the body, wrapped it in a clean linen cloth, ⁶⁰ and placed it in his own new tomb that he had cut out of the rock. He rolled a big stone in front of the entrance to the tomb and went away. ⁶¹ Mary Magdalene and the other Mary were sitting there opposite the tomb.*

Question: How do you feel when people will have to go and ask of your body?

8. Jesus' tomb guarded.

*⁶² The next day, the one after Preparation Day, the chief priests and the Pharisees went to Pilate. ⁶³ "Sir," they said, "we remember that while he was **still alive that deceiver** said, 'After three days I will rise again.' ⁶⁴ So give the order for the tomb to be made secure until the third day. Otherwise, his disciples may come and steal the body and tell the people that he has been raised from the dead. This last deception will be worse than the first." ⁶⁵ "Take a guard," Pilate answered. "Go, make the tomb as secure as you know how." ⁶⁶ So they went and made the tomb secure by putting a seal on the stone and posting the guard.*

Question: How does it feel like to be called a deceiver by the people you have come to save?

SUMMARY

1. How did Jesus respond to the gruesome treatment?

Jesus:

- Love
- Silence
- Respect
- Obedience
- Prayer/Fasting
- Openness
- Honesty
- Truth

2. How do we respond to gruesome treatment as His followers?

Let us follow Jesus way:

- Love
- Silence
- Respect
- Obedience
- Prayer/Fasting
- Openness
- Honesty
- Truth

THE LOVE SERMONS

7

CHRIST: THE ULTIMATE LOVE (PART 3)— LOVE RAISED HIM FROM THE DEAD

INTRODUCTION

Jesus' love is like no other. Love brought Him to earth, love made Him minister to all kinds of people, love made Him ride the donkey, love took Him to Gethsemane, love made Him endure arrest, mistreatment and death, but love raised Him from the dead and took Him back to heaven where, in love, He is interceding for us.

TEXTS

Matthew 28:1-20; Mark 16: 12-20; Luke 24: 36-53; Acts 1:9-11

After the Sabbath, at dawn on the first day of the week, Mary Magdalene and the other Mary went to look at the tomb. ² There was a violent earthquake, for an angel of the Lord came down from heaven and, going to the tomb, rolled back the stone and sat on it. ³ His appearance was like lightning, and his clothes were white as snow. ⁴ The guards were so afraid of him that they shook and became like dead men. ⁵ The angel said to the women, "Do not be afraid, for I know that you are looking for Jesus, who was crucified. ⁶ He is not here; he has risen, just as he said. Come and see the place where he *lay. ⁷ Then go quickly and tell his disciples: 'He has risen from the dead and is going ahead of you into Galilee. There you will see him.' Now I have told you." ⁸ So the women hurried away from the tomb, afraid yet filled with joy, and ran to tell his disciples. ⁹ **Suddenly Jesus met them.** "Greetings," he said. They came to him, clasped his feet, and worshiped him. ¹⁰ Then Jesus said to them, "Do not be afraid. Go and tell my brothers to go to Galilee; there they will see me." ¹¹ While the women were on their way, some of the guards went into the city and reported to the chief priests everything that had happened. ¹² When the chief priests had met with the elders and devised a plan, they gave the soldiers a large sum of money, ¹³ telling them, "You are to say, 'His disciples came during the night and stole him away while we were asleep.' ¹⁴ If this report gets to the governor, we will satisfy him and keep you out of trouble." ¹⁵ So the soldiers took the money and did as they were instructed. And this story has been widely circulated among the Jews to this very day. ¹⁶ Then the eleven disciples went to Galilee, to the mountain where Jesus had told them to go. ¹⁷ When they saw him, they worshiped him; but some doubted. ¹⁸ Then Jesus came to them and said, "All authority in heaven and on earth has been given to me. ¹⁹ Therefore go and make disciples of all nations, baptizing them in the name of the Father and of the Son and of the Holy Spirit, ²⁰ and teaching them to obey everything I have commanded you. And surely, I am with you always, to the very end of the age."*

Luke 24:50-53

⁵⁰ *When he had led them out to the vicinity of Bethany, he lifted up his hands and blessed them. ⁵¹ While he was blessing them, he left them and was taken up into heaven. ⁵² Then they worshiped him and*

returned to Jerusalem with great joy. *53 And they stayed continually at the temple, praising God.*

THE PURPOSE

For our time today is to remind us of EIGHT reasons we believe, Jesus is Risen and to trust in Him to live a resurrection life.

JESUS IS RISEN FROM THE DEAD:

WHY: Because:

1. The Women saw it.

After the Sabbath, at dawn on the first day of the week, Mary Magdalene and the other Mary went to look at the tomb. 8 So the women hurried away from the tomb, afraid yet filled with joy, and ran to tell his disciples.

2. The Angel confirmed it.

2 There was a violent earthquake, for an angel of the Lord came down from heaven and, going to the tomb, rolled back the stone and sat on it. 3 His appearance was like lightning, and his clothes were white as snow. 5 The angel said to the women, "Do not be afraid, for I know that you are looking for Jesus, who was crucified. 6 He is not here; he has risen, just as he said. Come and see the place where he lay. 7 Then go quickly and tell his disciples: 'He has risen from the dead and is going ahead of you into Galilee. There you will see him.' Now I have told you."

3. The Guards experienced it.

⁴ The guards were so afraid of him that they shook and became like dead men. ¹¹ While the women were on their way, **some of the guards** *went into the city and reported to the chief priests everything that had happened. ¹² When the chief priests had met with the elders and devised a plan, they gave the soldiers a large sum of money, ¹³ telling them, "You are to say, 'His disciples came during the night and stole him away while we were asleep.' ¹⁴ If this report gets to the governor, we will satisfy him and keep you out of trouble." ¹⁵ So the soldiers took the money and did as they were instructed. And this story has been widely circulated among the Jews to this very day.*

4. The risen Lord revealed it.

*⁹ **Suddenly Jesus met them.** "Greetings," he said. They came to him, clasped his feet, and worshiped him. ¹⁰ Then Jesus said to them, "Do not be afraid. Go and tell my brothers to go to Galilee; there they will see me."*

5. The two disciples on the way to Emmaus saw and ate with him.

¹² Afterward Jesus appeared in a different form to two of them while they were walking in the country. ¹³ These returned and reported it to the rest; but they did not believe them either.

6. The Eleven disciples saw, spoke, and ate with him.

¹⁶ Then the eleven disciples went to Galilee, to the mountain where Jesus had told them to go. ¹⁷ When they saw him, they worshiped him; but some doubted. ¹⁸ Then Jesus came to them and said, "All authority in heaven and on earth has been given to me.—Matthew 28:16-18

¹⁴ Later Jesus appeared to the Eleven as they were eating; he rebuked them for their lack of faith and their stubborn refusal to believe those who had seen him after he had risen.—Mark 16:14

³⁶ While they were still talking about this, Jesus himself stood among them and said to them, "Peace be with you." ³⁷ They were startled and frightened, thinking they saw a ghost. ³⁸ He said to them, "Why are you troubled, and why do doubts rise in your minds? ³⁹ Look at my hands and my feet. It is I myself! Touch me and see; a ghost does not have flesh and bones, as you see I have." ⁴⁰ When he had said this, he showed them his hands and feet. ⁴¹ And while they still did not believe it because of joy and amazement, he asked them, "Do you have anything here to eat?" ⁴² They gave him a piece of broiled fish, ⁴³ and he took it and ate it in their presence. ⁴⁴ He said to them, "This is what I told you while I was still with you: Everything must be fulfilled that is written about me in the Law of Moses, the Prophets and the Psalms."

7. The ascension confirms it.

¹⁹ After the Lord Jesus had spoken to them, he was taken up into heaven and he sat at the right hand of God.—Mark 16:19

⁹ After he said this, he was taken up before their very eyes, and a cloud hid him from their sight. ¹⁰ They were looking intently up into the sky as he was going, when suddenly two men dressed in white stood beside them. ¹¹ "Men of Galilee," they said, "why do you stand here looking into the sky? This same Jesus, who has been taken from you into heaven, will come back in the same way you have seen him go into heaven."—Acts 1:9-11.

⁵⁰ When he had led them out to the vicinity of Bethany, he lifted up his hands and blessed them. ⁵¹ While he was blessing them, he left them and was taken up into heaven. ⁵² Then they worshiped him and returned to Jerusalem with great joy. ⁵³ And they stayed continually at the temple, praising God.—Luke 24:50-53.

8. The believers of today affirm it.

¹⁹ Therefore go and make disciples of all nations, baptizing them in the name of the Father and of the Son and of the Holy Spirit, ²⁰ and teaching them to obey everything I have commanded you. And surely, I am with you always, to the very end of the age."—Matthew 28:16-20

¹⁵ He said to them, "Go into all the world and preach the gospel to all creation. ¹⁶ Whoever believes and is baptized will be saved, but whoever does not believe will be condemned. ¹⁷ And these signs will accompany those who believe: In my name they will drive out demons; they will speak in new tongues; ¹⁸ they will pick up snakes with their hands; and when they drink deadly poison, it will not hurt them at all; they will place their hands on sick people, and they will get well." Mark 16:15-18

²⁰ Then the disciples went out and preached everywhere, and the Lord worked with them and confirmed his word by the signs that accompanied it.—Mark 16:20

⁴⁵ Then he opened their minds so they could understand the Scriptures. ⁴⁶ He told them, "This is what is written: The Messiah will suffer and rise from the dead on the third day, ⁴⁷ and repentance for the forgiveness of sins will be preached in his name to all nations, beginning at Jerusalem. ⁴⁸ You are witnesses of these things. ⁴⁹ I am going to send you what my Father has promised; but stay in the city until you have been clothed with power from on high." —Luke 24:45-49.

Believers affirm it by:
- Faith in Christ
- Experience of forgiveness of sin
- Love for God and man
- Fruit we bear in season and out of season.
- Life we live—the changed lives. The transformed lives
- Signs and wonders through preaching

- The promise of the Father
- Hope we have in Christ and our future.

CONCLUSION

The Lord of Love is risen. Love raised Him from the dead. The women, the angel, the guards, the two, the eleven, the ascension and the believer today affirms it.

What He did, He is still doing it, will you let Him?

8

THE SPIRIT OF LOVE PRAYS
(LOVE IS THE SPIRIT OF PRAYER)

INTRODUCTION

The purpose is to encourage ourselves to know that our prayer life is an indication of our love for God.

QUESTIONS

- What is prayer?
- How important is prayer to you?
- Do you have a place, period and plan for prayer?
- When did you pray last week? And when will you pray this week?
- Why must you pray? And why do you pray?

Isaiah 56:7: New American Standard Bible

7 Even those I will bring to My holy mountain, And make them joyful in My house of prayer. Their burnt offerings and their sacrifices will be acceptable on My altar; For My house will be called a house of prayer for all the peoples."

Jeremiah 7:11: New American Standard Bible
¹¹ Has this house, which is called by My name, become a den of robbers in your sight? Behold, I Myself have seen it," declares the LORD.

Matthew 21:13: New American Standard Bible
¹³ And He said to them, "It is written: 'MY HOUSE WILL BE CALLED A HOUSE OF PRAYER'; but you are making it a DEN OF ROBBERS."

Mark 11:17: New American Standard Bible
¹⁷ And He began to teach and say to them, "Is it not written: 'MY HOUSE WILL BE CALLED A HOUSE OF PRAYER FOR ALL THE NATIONS'? But you have made it a DEN OF ROBBERS."

ILLUSTRATIONS

1. LUKE 18:1-8

"Then Jesus told his disciples a parable to show them that they should always pray and not give up. ² He said: "In a certain town there was **a judge who neither feared God nor cared what people thought.** *³ And there was **a widow** in that town who kept coming to him with the plea,* **'Grant me justice against my adversary.'** *⁴ "For some time he refused. But finally, he said to himself, 'Even though I do not fear God or care what people think, ⁵ yet because this widow* **keeps bothering me,** *I will see that she gets justice, so that she won't eventually come and attack me!'" ⁶ And the Lord said, "Listen to what the unjust judge says. ⁷* **And will not God bring about justice for his chosen ones, who cry out to him day and night?** *Will he keep putting them off? ⁸ I tell you; he will see that they get justice, and*

quickly. However, when the Son of Man comes, will he find faith on the earth?"

Luke 11:5-8 (NIV)

⁵ Then Jesus said to them, "Suppose you have a friend, and you go to him at midnight and say, 'Friend, lend me three loaves of bread; ⁶ a friend of mine on a journey has come to me, and I have no food to offer him.' ⁷ And suppose the one inside answers, 'Do not bother me. The door is already locked, and my children and I are in bed. I can't get up and give you anything.' ⁸ I tell you, even though he will not get up and give you the bread because of friendship, yet because of your shameless audacity he will surely get up and give you as much as you need.

What does pray and not faint mean?

The Lord adds another important phrase. He said that we are **not** to **faint**. The word has the **meaning** of becoming discouraged, or to lose heart, to despair, to tire through weariness of spirit.

Some have lost heart and look **no** more for the promise of his coming. Some have lost jobs; some have lost family. Some have lost money. Some have lost a relationship.

What does the parable of the persistent friend teach us?

- The need to have a friend and to be a friend.
- The need to always pray. (morning, noon, evening, midnight)—cry out day and night.
- The need to never ever give up praying.

- The need to have a shameless audacity.
- The need to know the God you love, serve, and obey.
- The need to draw closer to God.

2. LUKE 18:9-14

*⁹ He also told this parable to **some** who trusted in themselves that they were righteous, and treated others with contempt: ¹⁰ "Two men went up into the temple to pray, one a Pharisee and the other a tax collector. ¹¹ The **Pharisee**, standing by himself, prayed thus: 'God, I thank you that I am not like other men, extortioners, unjust, adulterers, or even like this tax collector. ¹² I fast twice a week; I give tithes of all that I get.' ¹³ But the **tax collector**, standing far off, would not even lift up his eyes to heaven, but beat his breast, saying, 'God, be merciful to me, a sinner!' ¹⁴ I tell you; this man went down to his house justified, rather than the other. For everyone who exalts himself will be humbled, but the one who humbles himself will be exalted."*

The Spirit of Love in the Spirit of Prayer:

- Does not trust in self.
- Is not self righteous.
- Does not treat others with disrespect.
- Is exalted through the spirit of humility.

CONCLUSION

The Spirit of Love is indeed the Spirit of prayer that is prayed out daily with the Spirit of humility and persistence because of faith, trust, hope and love for God.

Small Group Lesson: THE SPIRIT OF LOVE PRAYS

Even those I will bring to My holy mountain, And make them joyful in My house of prayer. Their burnt offerings and their sacrifices will be acceptable on My altar; For My house will be called a house of prayer for all the peoples.".

~ Isaiah 56:7 (NASB)

INTRODUCTION – Prayer makes a godly man, and puts within him the mind of Christ, the mind of humility, of self-surrender, of service, of pity, and of prayer. If we really pray, we will become more like God, or else we will quit praying. The Spirit of Love is indeed the Spirit of prayer that is prayed out with the Spirit of humility and persistent daily because of faith, trust, hope and love for God.

TALK IT OVER

Concerning prayer, Jesus does not suggest but Commands us to Pray.

1. Therefore, Believers Must…

   • Always PRAY
     Pray without ceasing, 18 give thanks in all circumstances; for this is the will of God in Christ Jesus for you – **1 Thes 5:17-18**

   • Not Give Up In PRAYER and be PERSISTENT

Be persistent and devoted to prayer, being alert and focused in your prayer life with an attitude of thanksgiving. -Col 4:2 (**Amp**)

- **Not Be Easily DISCOURAGED**
  But they who wait for the Lord shall renew their strength; They shall mount up with wings like eagles; They shall run and not be weary; They shall walk and not faint.
  -Isai 40:31

2. **Praying in the Spirit of LOVE Means....**

- **You must not depend on or trust in yourself, but in GOD**
  Trust in the Lord with all your heart, and lean not on your own understanding   –
  Prov 3:5

- **You Must not walk in SELF-RIGHTEOUSNESS**
  All the ways of a man are clean in his own sight, But the Lord weighs the motives.   –
  Prov 16:2

- **You Must RESPECT others**
  Do nothing out of selfish ambition or vain conceit. Rather, in humility value others above yourselves
  – Phil 2:3

- **You Must walk in HUMILITY.**
  For all those who exalt themselves will be humbled, and those who humble themselves will be exalted.   -
  Luke 14:11

DISCOVERY QUESTIONS

1. How important is prayer to you and why do you pray?

2. Do you have a place, period, and plan for prayer?

PRAYER DIRECTION

1. Dear God, please make me a Christian that loves other people with all my heart. Help me to have a selfless attitude towards others.

2. Dear Jesus Christ, please empower me to have compassion for needy people. Let me express my faith in you by loving other people.

9

THE SPIRIT OF LOVE CELEBRATES

TEXTS

1 Corinthians 5:1-13 Proverbs 3:5-6; Isaiah 48:17-21; Isaiah 45:1-7

PURPOSE

The purpose is to remind us that our submission and willingness to love God, and love people through genuine celebration assures us of God's power, presence, prosperity, and provision.

The Spirit of Love celebrates with Confidence in the confidence of God.

A. LET US BEGIN WITH WHAT AND HOW:

It is actually reported that there is sexual immorality among you, and of a kind that is not tolerated even among pagans, for a man has his father's wife. ² And you are arrogant! Ought you not rather to mourn? Let him who has done this be removed from among you. ³ For though absent in body, I am present in spirit; and as if present, I have already pronounced judgment on the one who did such a thing. ⁴ When you *are assembled in the name of the Lord Jesus and my spirit is present, with the power of our Lord Jesus, ⁵ you are to deliver this man to Satan for the destruction of the flesh, so that his spirit may be saved in the day of the Lord. ⁶ Your boasting is not good. Do you not know that a little leaven leavens the whole lump? ⁷ Cleanse out the old leaven that you may be a new lump, as you really are unleavened. For Christ, our Passover lamb, has been sacrificed. ⁸ **Let us therefore celebrate the festival, not with the old leaven, the leaven of malice and evil, but with the unleavened bread of sincerity and truth.** ⁹ I wrote to you in my letter not to associate with sexually immoral people— ¹⁰ not at all meaning the sexually immoral of this world, or the greedy and swindlers, or idolaters, since then you would need to go out of the world. ¹¹ But now I am writing to you not to associate with anyone who bears the name of brother if he is guilty of sexual immorality or greed, or is an idolater, reviler, drunkard, or swindler—not even to eat with such a one. ¹² For what have I to do with judging outsiders? Is it not those inside the church whom you are to judge? ¹³ God judges those outside. "Purge the evil person from among you."*

Celebration with a heart filled with:

1. **Sincerity:** *Definition*—Not dishonest, heartfelt, hearty, genuine in feeling, wholehearted. Free from pretense or deceit. It stresses the absence of hypocrisy. Giving compliments, gratitude that reflects your true inner feelings.
2. **Truth:** *Definition*—Is what is true, everything that is true.

B. LET US CONTINUE WITH WHY AND WHO

Celebrate with Confidence.

Proverbs 3:5-6

My son do not forget my teaching, but keep my commands in your heart, ²for they will prolong your life many years and bring you peace and prosperity. ³ **Let love and faithfulness never leave you; bind them around your neck, write them on the tablet of your heart.** *⁴ Then you will win favor and a good name in the sight of God and man. ⁵* **Trust in the LORD with all your heart and lean not on your own understanding; ⁶ in all your ways submit to him, and he will make your paths straight.** *⁷ Do not be wise in your own eyes; fear the LORD and shun evil. ⁸ This will bring health to your body and nourishment to your bones. ⁹ Honor the LORD with your wealth, with the first fruits of all your crops; ¹⁰ then your barns will be filled to overflowing, and your vats will brim over with new wine.*

1. **Let us not lean on our own understanding in following the path of Love.**

Isaiah 48:17-21

This is what the LORD says—your Redeemer, the Holy One of Israel: "I am the LORD your God, who **teaches** *you what is best for you,* **who directs you** *in the way you should go. ¹⁸ If only you had paid attention to my commands, your peace would have been like a river, your well-being like the waves of the sea. ¹⁹ Your descendants would have been like the sand, your children like its numberless grains; their name would never be blotted out nor destroyed from before me." ²⁰ Leave Babylon, flee from the Babylonians! Announce this with shouts of joy and proclaim it. Send it out to the ends of the earth; say, "The*

LORD *has redeemed his servant Jacob.*" *²¹ They did* **not thirst when** *he led them through the deserts; he made water flow for them from the rock; he split the rock and water gushed out.*

2. The leading of the Lord guarantees His supply.

Isaiah 45:1-7

"This is what the LORD *says to his anointed, to Cyrus, whose right hand I take hold of to subdue nations before him and to strip kings of their armor, to open doors before him so that gates will not be shut:* ² **I will go before you and will level the mountains**[a]**; I will break down gates of bronze and cut through bars of iron.** ³ **I will give you hidden treasures, riches stored in secret places, so that you may know that I am the** LORD**, the God of Israel, who summons you by name.** ⁴ *For the sake of Jacob my servant, of Israel my chosen, I summon you by name and bestow on you a title of honor, though you do not acknowledge me.* ⁵ **I am the** LORD**, and there is no other; apart from me there is no God. I will strengthen you, though you have not acknowledged me,** ⁶ *so that from the rising of the sun to the place of its setting people may know there is none besides me. I am the* LORD*, and there is no other.* ⁷ *I form the light and create darkness, I bring prosperity and create disaster; I, the* LORD*, do all these things.*

3. Follow the Lord daily and completely in love Him with your all.

Deuteronomy 2:24-25

²⁴ Moses continued, "Then the LORD said, 'Now get moving! Cross the Arnon Gorge. Look, I will hand over to you Sihon the Amorite, king of Heshbon, and I will give you his land. Attack him and begin to occupy the land. ²⁵ Beginning today I will make people throughout the earth terrified because of you. When they hear reports about you, they will tremble with dread and fear.'"

4. Love God and fight to love others like Christ did.

CONCLUSION

Live a life of Love in sincerity, truth, following the leading of God, fight on your knees to always love and in all circumstances.

10

LOVE MAKES DISCIPLES (PART 1)— WHAT AND WHO IS A DISCIPLE?

TEXT:

Matthew 28:18-20

¹⁸ Then Jesus came to them and said, "All authority in heaven and on earth has been given to me. ¹⁹ Therefore go and make disciples of all nations, baptizing them in the name of the Father and of the Son and of the Holy Spirit, ²⁰ and teaching them to obey everything I have commanded you. And surely, I am with you always, to the very end of the age."

QUESTIONS:

- What is disciple, disciple-making, discipleship?
- Who is a disciple?
- How do I stay a disciple?

The Christian church has taken this command very seriously, but what does it mean to the uninitiated? What does it mean to *be* a disciple of Christ, much less to *make* more disciples?

WHAT IS IT?

Wikipedia says it this way: "In Christianity, disciple primarily refers to a dedicated follower of Jesus."

"To be a learner" is the literal answer to the question, "What is a discipleship definition?"

Dictionary.com defines a disciple as:
- A person who is a pupil or adherent to the doctrines of another.
- One who embraces and assists in spreading the teaching of another.
- Any follower of another person.

"Disciple" is a word that is not generally considered a part of everyday vocabulary in contemporary society, but it gets tossed around a lot in Christian circles. You might hear phrases like: *"called to be disciples of Christ," "make disciples of all nations," "walk as a disciple."* The concept seems very intimidating, and to a person who has not spent a lifetime in church, but who wants to know God, it can be confusing. In one way or another, we are all disciples already. We may not necessarily be disciples of Christ or of the Christian faith, but we are disciples of something. Maybe you have a favorite writer, or a sports star that you grew up trying to emulate. Perhaps there is a person that you work with that you try to learn from. Maybe it is something else. But whatever it is, each of us is already a disciple.

In the Bible, Christ's final command to His followers is to *"Therefore, as you go, disciple people in all nations, baptizing them in the name of the Father, and the Son, and the Holy Spirit"* (Matthew 28:19).

What Do We Mean by "Disciple," "Disciple Making," and "Discipleship"? (discipleship.org)

Words matter. Definitions matter, especially with regard to words and concepts we find in Scripture. A particular word may carry different definitions and meanings, depending on one's perspective, and this is true for discipleship language.

That means we can use the same language about discipleship as someone else, and each of us be talking about totally different things.

But what does God's Word say? And how do our definitions line up with his realities? This is an important discussion for discipleship and disciple making, so at Discipleship.org, we worked with our partners to agree upon specific definitions for important words in the church.

We must be clear on definitions so that we can be clear on our success.

That is why we offer these four key definitions for the church today:

1. **Disciple**—someone who is following Jesus, being changed by Jesus, and is committed to the mission of Jesus (Matt. 4:19).

2. **Disciple making**—entering into relationships to **help people trust and follow Jesus** (Matt. 28:18–20), which includes the whole process from conversion through maturation and multiplication.

3. **Disciple maker**—a disciple of Jesus who enters into relationships with people to help them trust and follow Jesus.

4. **Discipleship**—the state of being a disciple.

CHANGING FROM THE INSIDE: IT HAS TO DO WITH CHANGE. CHANGED OF LIFE.

The important distinction with Christian discipleship is that we are not only called to learn the teachings of Jesus Christ, but we are also called to live them. A disciple who bases his or her life on the teachings of Christ *"like a person building a house, who dug a deep hole to lay the foundation on rock"* (Luke 6:48).

When we make our initial declaration of faith and ask Christ to be our Savior, He will begin changing us from the inside, giving us the ability to understand His word and the desire to live it.

HOW DOES GOD CHANGE US FROM THE INSIDE?

> **The Word Factor:**
   As we read God's Word, we learn about Jesus and how He lived. We begin to understand what it means to be like

Jesus. We learn to put Him first in all things (Mark 8:34-38).

34 Then he called the crowd to him along with his disciples and said: "Whoever wants to be my disciple must deny themselves and take up their cross and follow me. 35 For whoever wants to save their life[a] will lose it, but whoever loses their life for me and for the gospel will save it. 36 What good is it for someone to gain the whole world, yet forfeit their soul? 37 Or what can anyone give in exchange for their soul? 38 If anyone is ashamed of me and my words in this adulterous and sinful generation, the Son of Man will be ashamed of them when he comes in his Father's glory with the holy angels."

- ➢ **The Holy Spirit Factor:**
  We become equipped to listen to the Holy Spirit, who lives within us. He helps us resist temptation and overcome trials (Ephesians 6:10-18).

10 Finally, be strong in the Lord and in his mighty power. 11 Put on the full armor of God, so that you can take your stand against the devil's schemes. 12 For our struggle is not against flesh and blood, but against the rulers, against the authorities, against the powers of this dark world and against the spiritual forces of evil in the heavenly realms. 13 Therefore put on the full armor of God, so that when the day of evil comes, you may be able to stand your ground, and after you have done everything, to stand. 14 Stand firm then, with the belt of truth buckled around your waist, with the breastplate of righteousness in place, 15 and with your feet fitted with the readiness that comes from the gospel of peace. 16 In addition to all this, take up the shield of faith, with which you can extinguish all the flaming arrows of the evil one. ¹⁷ Take the helmet of salvation and the sword of the Spirit, which is the word of God. ¹⁸ And pray in the Spirit on all occasions with all kinds of prayers and requests. With this in mind, be alert and always keep on praying for all the Lord's people.

> **The Action Factor:**
We learn how to examine our thoughts, actions, and words—always comparing them with Scripture. We want to be doers of the Word, and not hearers only (James 1:22).

²² Do not merely listen to the word, and so deceive yourselves. Do what it says.

> **The Abide Factor:**
We begin to understand what it means to "abide in Christ." As we abide, the Holy Spirit produces fruit in our lives—love, joy, peace, patience, kindness, goodness, faithfulness, gentleness, and self-control. These are not things we can conjure up on our own. They are produces by the Holy Spirit—a change from the inside out (Galatians 5:22-23).

²² But the fruit of the Spirit is love, joy, peace, forbearance, kindness, goodness, faithfulness, ²³ gentleness and self-control. Against such things there is no law.

> **The Love Factor:**
We start loving other people through action (John 13:35).

³⁵ By this everyone will know that you are my disciples if you love one another."

> ## The Sharing Factor:
> We long to share our faith with others and tell unbelievers about the changes Jesus has made in our lives (1 Peter 3:15).

¹⁵ But in your hearts revere Christ as Lord. Always be prepared to give an answer to everyone who asks you to give the reason for the hope that you have. But do this with gentleness and respect,

And while it is true that when we become Christians, we are called to make disciples of others, we must remember that discipleship has to start somewhere. Nobody becomes a disciple-maker overnight. God knows our hearts; He understands that we are going to have to take baby steps to get from point A to point B. So, do not let all that **"make disciples"** talk frighten you away from seeking Christ and becoming His disciple. Remember that with the power of God on our side, we are capable of so much more than we could ever imagine. "Those who know your name will trust you for you have not forsaken those who seek you, LORD" (Psalm 9:10). The defining trait of any Christian disciple is faith. Faith in God will give us the power to become disciples, and to make more disciples by leading others to faith.

5 QUESTIONS TO ASK DAILY AS A LIVING DISCIPLE.

1. Who should I pray for? Ask God for wisdom and insight

We cannot even begin to direct our mindset towards spiritual things without the help of the Holy Spirit. The default human mindset does not automatically think of others and their needs first.

"Do not conform to the pattern of this world but be transformed by the renewing of your mind. Then you will be able to test and approve what God's will is—his good, pleasing and perfect will." Romans 12:2

"If any of you lacks wisdom, you should ask God, who gives generously to all without finding fault, and it will be given to you". James 1:5

2. Who is missing?

Sometimes we get so caught up in our busy lives that people we care about may fall off the grid without our noticing.

"Suppose one of you has a hundred sheep and loses one of them. Doesn't he leave the ninety-nine in the open country and go after the lost sheep until he finds it? Luke 15:4

3. Who can I serve?

As you go through your day, look around and try to take notice of who you could serve through your actions or your words.

"Therefore, as we have opportunity, let us do good to all people, especially to those who belong to the family of believers." Galatians 6:10

4. Who can I invite to go with me?

When Jesus was here on the earth, he was always inviting his disciples to go places with him. To weddings, to funerals, to impromptu picnic's where he provided the food – Then when he began to send his disciples out to do ministry without him, he sent them in pairs. Discipleship is really better caught than taught. Every time we go 'do' something it is an opportunity to either model some aspect of discipleship to someone we are leading, or to go deeper in relationship with someone we are getting to know.

"Calling the Twelve to him, he began to send them out two by two and gave them authority over impure spirits." Mark 6:7

5. Who can I tell about my life with Jesus?

It can sometimes be intimidating to think about sharing "The Gospel"—but the meaning of that term in the Bible is actually "Good News". And I do not know about you, but most people do not have a problem sharing good news with each other.

"Return home and tell how much God has done for you." So, the man went away and told all over town how much Jesus had done for him.—Luke 8:39

"But in your hearts revere Christ as Lord. Always be prepared to give an answer to everyone who asks you to give the reason for the hope that you have. But do this with gentleness and respect"—1 Peter 3:15

CONCLUSION

- Be a disciple and keep making disciples.

Small Group Lesson: LOVE MAKES DISCIPLES – What and who is a Disciple?

18 Then Jesus came to them and said, "All authority in heaven and on earth has been given to me. 19 Therefore go and make disciples of all nations, baptizing them in the name of the Father and of the Son and of the Holy Spirit, 20 and teaching them to obey everything I have commanded you. And surely, I am with you always, to the very end of the age." ~Matthew 28:18-20

INTRODUCTION – When the church becomes an end in itself, it ends. When Sunday school, as great as it is, becomes an end in itself, it ends. When small groups ministry becomes an end in itself, it ends. When the worship service becomes an end in itself, it ends. What we need is for discipleship to become the goal, and then the process never ends. The process is fluid. It is moving. It is active. It is a living thing. It must continue to go on. Every disciple must make disciples."

— Robby Gallaty.

TALK IT OVER

Let's Discuss These Definitions...

1. **A Disciple** – Is someone who is following Jesus, being changed by Jesus, and is committed to the mission of Jesus (*Matt. 4:19*).

2. **Disciple Making** – Is entering into relationships to help people trust and follow Jesus, which includes the whole process from conversion, maturation and multiplication. (*Matt. 28:18–20*)

3. **Disciple Maker** – A disciple of Jesus who enters into relationships with people to help them trust and follow Jesus.

4. **Discipleship** – Is the state of being a disciple.

How to become a DISCIPLE and a DISCIPLE MAKER:

1. **The Word Factor:** As we read God's Word, we learn about Jesus, how He lived and to put him first in all things (*Mk 8:34-38).

2. **The Holy Spirit Factor:** We become equipped to listen to the Holy Spirit in us, to resist temptation and overcome trials (*Eph 6:10-18*).

3. *The Action Factor:* We learn how to examine our thoughts, actions, and words with Scripture. (*James 1:22*).

4. *The Abide Factor:* We begin to understand what it means to "abide in Christ and to produce fruits (*Gal 5:22-23*).

5. **The Love Factor:** We start loving other people through action *(John 13:35)*
6. **The Sharing Factor:** We long to share our faith with others and tell unbelievers about the changes Jesus has made in our lives *(1 Pet 3:15)*

DISCOVERY QUESTIONS

1. Jesus intentionally made disciples. Why are we not making disciples?

2. Why is it important for believers to be discipled and to be making disciples?

PRAYER DIRECTION

1. Dear God, empower our congregations to actively and successfully engage in making disciples of Jesus Christ. *Matt. 28:19*

2. God, provide opportunities for personal growth and spiritual formation that strengthen our members in their Christian walk. *1 Thess. 3:13*

11

LOVE MAKES DISCIPLES (PART 2)—DISCIPLES SERVE IN LOVE

TEXTS:

Matthew 20:20-28; Mark 10:35-45; John 13:1-17

A MOTHER'S PLEA!

20 Then the wife of Zebedee came to Jesus with her sons. She bowed before him and asked him to do something for her. 21 Jesus asked, "What do you want?" She said, "Promise that one of my sons will sit at your right side and the other will sit at your left side in your kingdom." 22 But Jesus said, "You don't understand what you are asking. Can you drink the cup that I am about to drink?" The sons answered, "Yes, we can." 23 Jesus said to them, "You will drink from my cup. But I cannot choose who will sit at my right or my left; those places belong to those for whom my Father has prepared them." 24 When the other ten followers heard this, they were angry with the two brothers. 25 Jesus called all the followers together and said, "You know that the rulers of the non-Jewish people love to show their power over the people. And their important leaders love to use all their authority. 26 But it should not be that way among you. Whoever wants to become great among you must serve the rest of you like a servant. 27 Whoever wants to become first among you must serve the rest of you like a slave.

²⁸ In the same way, the Son of Man did not come to be served. He came to serve others and to give his life as a ransom for many people."

WHAT?

In part 1 we learnt that **A Disciple of Christ** is one who believes in the Gospel of Christ to change his life and trusts Christ by the same means of the Gospel to change their lives to live like Christ on earth.

1. Disciple Based on Matthew 4:19 by Jim Putman

"And he said to them, follow me, and I will make you fishes of men" ESV.

1. Following Jesus (Head)
2. Being changed by Jesus through the Holy Spirit (Heart)
3. "Fishers of Men" Being committed to the mission of Christ (Hands).

A disciple is following Jesus, being changed by Jesus, and committed to the Mission of Jesus.
A living disciple loves Jesus, loves People, lives the word, and reaches the world.

2. As a disciple or Living disciple:

What do you say or tell yourself when you hear of the call to serve?

We make all sorts of rational explanations for not serving:
- I do not have time.
- I do not know what I would do.
- I am afraid of the virus and the variants.
- I do not have any special skills to contribute.
- I do not have the money to do it.
- They do not need me.

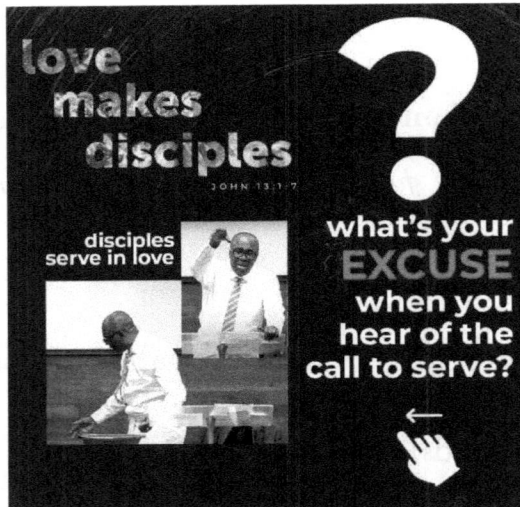

But the reality is the Lord does not call the equipped; He equips the called. God used men and women with similar doubts to change the course of history. Moses did not think he was a leader or speaker, but God worked through Moses to bring Israel out of slavery. Saul, the first King of Israel hid himself when they needed him to serve as King. But...David was the youngest (and therefore most insignificant) of all his brothers, but God worked through David to defeat a giant and eventually made him a king. Paul used to kill Christians before he met Jesus, but he went on to become one of the most highly regarded and prolific writers, disciple-makers, leadership developers and church planters in history.

Note: When it comes to service, God will if you are willing.

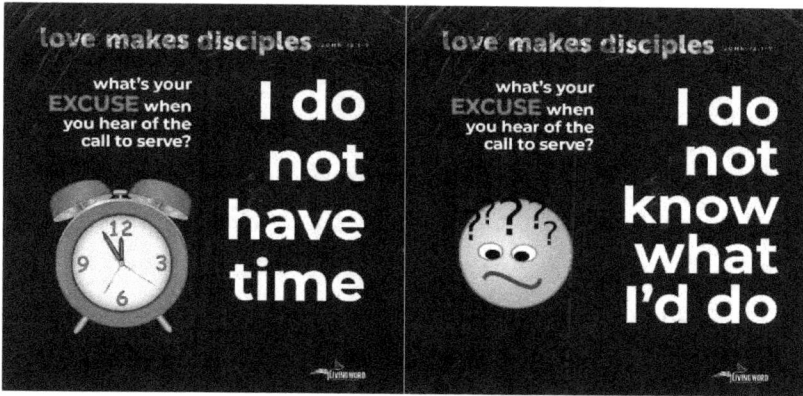

HOW?

Follow the Example of Jesus

Every Christian is expected to serve. God has equipped each of us with talents, skills, and spiritual gifts. God desires for us to use the various gifts He has given us to serve. When we serve, we are following in the footsteps of Jesus. We also grow in spiritual maturity and please God when we make serving in the church a priority in our lives.

3. Let us look at what Jesus did with serving.

It was just before the Passover Festival. Jesus knew that the hour had come for him to leave this world and go to the Father. Having loved his own who were in the world, he loved them to the end. ² The evening meal was in progress, and the devil had already prompted Judas, the son of Simon Iscariot, to betray Jesus. ³ Jesus knew that the Father had put all things under his power, and that he had come from God and was returning to God; ⁴ so he got up from the meal, took off his outer clothing, and wrapped a towel around his waist. ⁵ After that, he poured water into a basin and began to wash his disciples' feet, drying them with the towel that was wrapped around him. ⁶ He came to Simon Peter, who said to him, "Lord, are you going to wash my feet?" ⁷ Jesus replied, "You do not realize now what I am doing, but later you will understand." ⁸ "No," said Peter, "you shall never wash my feet." Jesus answered, "Unless I wash you, you have no part with me." ⁹ "Then, Lord," Simon Peter replied, "not just my feet but my hands and my head as well!" ¹⁰ Jesus answered, "Those who have had a bath need only to wash their feet; their whole body is clean. And you are clean, though not every one of you." ¹¹ For he knew who was going to betray him, and that was why he said not everyone was clean. ¹² When he had finished washing their feet, he put on his clothes and returned to his place. "Do you understand what I have done for you?" he asked them. ¹³ "You call me 'Teacher' and 'Lord,' and rightly so, for that is what I am. ¹⁴ Now that I, your Lord and Teacher, have washed your feet, you also should wash one another's feet. ¹⁵ I have set you an example that you should do as I have done for you. ¹⁶ Very truly I tell you, no servant is greater than his master, nor is a messenger greater than the one who sent him. [17] Now that you know these things, you will be blessed if you do them.

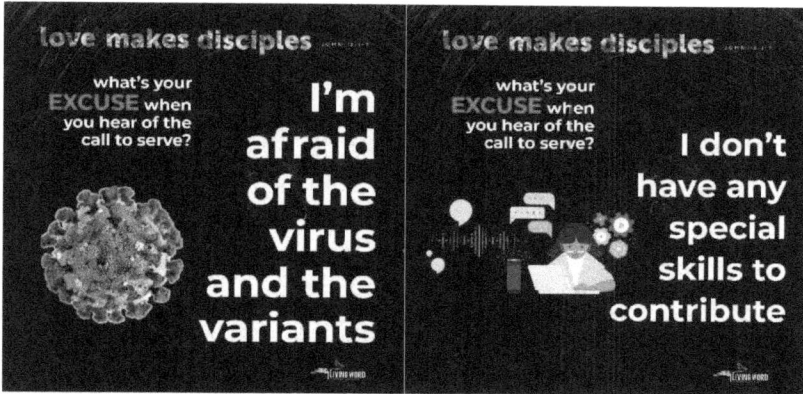

QUESTIONS:

1. Was Jesus just being practical when washing the disciples' feet, or was He trying to teach a spiritual lesson? What do you think?
   - ➤ **Teaching servant leadership**

2. What did Jesus mean when He said we should wash one another's feet?
   - ➤ **We should cultivate an attitude and approach to life that puts others first in verse 17**

3. What did Jesus say would bring a blessing?

   Obedience to Him and His Word John 12:26 says *"Whoever serves me must follow me; and where I am, my servant also will be. My Father will honor the one who serves me."*

4. Whose example did Jesus say we must follow?

His

^{15} I have set you an example that you should do as I have done for you.

5. Who did Jesus say the Father would honour?
Those that serve Jesus.

^{17} Now that you know these things, you will be blessed if you do them.

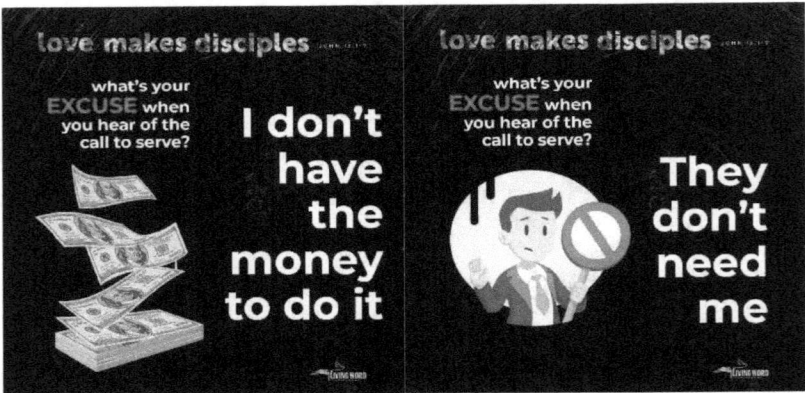

4. Let us look at what Jesus said about serving:

Mark 10:42-45

^{35} Then James and John, the sons of Zebedee, came to him. "Teacher," they said, "we want you to do for us whatever we ask." ^{36} "What do you want me to do for you?" he asked. ^{37} They replied, "Let one of us sit at your right and the other at your left in your glory." ^{38} "You don't know what you are asking," Jesus said. "Can you drink the cup I

drink or be baptized with the baptism I am baptized with?" [39] *"We can," they answered. Jesus said to them, "You will drink the cup I drink and be baptized with the baptism I am baptized with,* [40] *but to sit at my right or left is not for me to grant. These places belong to those for whom they have been prepared."* [41] *When the ten heard about this, they became indignant with James and John.* [42] *Jesus called them together and said, "You know that those who are regarded as rulers of the Gentiles lord it over them, and their high officials exercise authority over them.* [43] *Not so with you. Instead, whoever wants to become great among you must be your servant,* [44] *and whoever wants to be first must be slave of all.* [45] *For even the Son of Man did not come to be served, but to serve, and to give his life as a ransom for many."*

QUESTIONS:

1. How does one become great in God's eyes?
   ➢ Serve others gladly—Jesus is our example.

2. Did Jesus come to serve or be served?
   ➢ He came to serve-we need to do the same.

3. What important lesson can we learn from this passage?
   ➢ Serve like Christ.
   ➢ Put God first,
   ➢ Put others before you.
   ➢ Relate well, treat well, love well.
   ➢ Have a proper attitude and the right motive.

CONCLUSION

- ➤ Let us make time to use the gifts and talents God has provided us with to serve Him through the local church and the world.

- ➤ God desires that we place Him first in our lives. Part of this means taking time to serve.

- ➤ We grow spiritually when we follow in the footsteps of Jesus and make serving others an important part of our lives. God will bless you as you bless others in serving.

12

LOVE MAKES DISCIPLES (PART 3)—A DISCIPLE SHARES THE FAITH IN LOVE

First of all, then, I urge that supplications, prayers, intercessions, and thanksgivings be made for all people, 2 for kings and all who are in high positions, that we may lead a peaceful and quiet life, godly and dignified in every way. 3 This is good, and it is pleasing in the sight of God our Savior, 4 who desires all people to be saved and to come to the knowledge of the truth.—1 Timothy 2:1-4 ESV

TEXTS:

Luke 9:1-6; 10:1-21; Matthew 28:18-20; John 6:44

Luke 9:1-6 New Life Version

Jesus called His twelve followers to Him. He gave them the right and the power over all demons and to heal diseases. ² He sent them to preach about the holy nation of God and to heal the sick. ³ Then He said to them, "Take nothing along for the trip. Do not take a walking stick or a bag or bread or money. Do not take two coats. ⁴ Whatever house you go into, stay there until you are ready to go on. ⁵ If anyone will not take you in, as you leave that city, shake its dust off your feet. That will speak against them." ⁶ They went out, going from town to town. They preached the Good News and healed the sick everywhere.

Luke 10:1-11, 17-21 New Life Version.

*After this the Lord chose seventy others. He sent them out two together to every city and place where He would be going later. ² Jesus said to them, "There is much grain ready to gather. But the workmen are few. Pray then to the Lord Who is the Owner of the grain-fields that He will send workmen to gather His grain. ³ Go on your way. Listen! I send you out like lambs among wolves. ⁴ Take no money. Do not take a bag or shoes. Speak to no one along the way. ⁵ When you go into a house, say that you hope peace will come to them. ⁶ If a man who loves peace lives there, your good wishes will come to him. If your good wishes are not received, they will come back to you. ⁷ Stay in the same house. Eat and drink what they give you. The workman should have his thanks. Do not move from house to house. ⁸ "Whenever a city receives you, eat the things that are put before you there. ⁹ Heal the sick. Say to them, 'The holy nation of God is near.' ¹⁰ Whatever city does not receive you, go into its streets and say, ¹¹ 'Even the dust of your city that is on our feet we are cleaning off against you. But understand this, **the holy nation of God has come near you!'** ¹⁷ The seventy came back full of joy. They said, "Lord, even the demons obeyed us when we used Your name." ¹⁸ Jesus said to them, "I saw Satan fall from heaven like lightning. ¹⁹ Listen! I have given you power to walk on snakes. I have given you power over small animals with a sting of poison. I have given you power over all the power of the one who works against you. Nothing will hurt you. ²⁰ Even so, you should not be happy because the demons obey you but be happy because your names are written in heaven." ²¹ At this time Jesus was full of the joy of the Holy Spirit. He said, "I thank You, Father, Lord of heaven and earth. You have kept these things hidden from the wise* *and from those who have much learning. You have shown them to little children. Yes, Father, it was what you wanted done.*

OUTLINE

1. Questions.
2. Jesus' Mission, Power, Method, Message, and Meaning.
3. What the sharing of our faith involves.
4. How Scripture wants us to share our faith.

Sharing our faith with others is part of the Christian life. Sharing our faith in the way Jesus teaches and desires us to, yields maximum results. Sharing our faith in Jesus is done in obedience to the great commission. Jesus instructed His followers to go into all the world and make disciples.

Note:

Proclaiming the gospel—While it is true that we are witnesses to others through our lifestyles, we can also take the initiative and share the Gospel with others verbally. Share by Deed and Words.

1. Let us ask and answer some questions.

➢ What does the Bible say about sharing our faith?
➢ What is the mission of the church according to Jesus?
➢ What needs to happen for a person to come to Jesus?
➢ Who does God want to see saved? **1 Timothy 2:1-4**
➢ What does it mean to be salt and light?

➤ Who is sinful and falls short of God's glory? Romans 3:23; 6:23; John 3:16-21

➤ What motivated God to give His Son? Who did God give His Son for? What standing do people have before God if they do not believe in Jesus?

➤ Why do people refuse to come to Jesus? Acts 17:29-31.

➤ Who does God call to repent?

➤ What gift do we receive when we place faith in Christ? Romans 5:17

➤ What is your story? Who can you Share it with today? (story) Acts 26:1-29

➤ Who can you invite to Jesus?

Note:

To be salt and light—When it comes to sharing our faith, we are not only called to go out and witness. We are also called to be witnesses through the transformed lives that we live. Matthew 5:13-16

2. Let us look at the Jesus plan:

- Incarnate - Jesus came into our world to show us God's love.
- Select– People were Jesus' method.
- Associate – Jesus stayed with them.
- Consecrate – Jesus required obedience.
- Demonstrate – Jesus showed them how to live.

- Delegate – Jesus assigned them work.
- Supervise – Jesus continued to check on them.
- Reproduce– Jesus expected them to reproduce.
- Impart – Jesus gave Himself away (through the Holy Spirit).

I believe that Jesus intended for us to adopt His plan. He simply asked His disciples to do for others what He had done for them. He knew what He was doing, and God will bless church leaders who seek to replicate His plan today.

3. Let us see what is involved in Sharing our Jesus Story.

- Every Believer
- All Nations
- All churches
- Need More Workers
- Requires more Prayers.
- Absolute Dependence on God
- Brings persecution.
- Demands Living the story we share.
- Relationship Driven
- Being a servant
- Contextual but Countercultural.

4. Let us find out How to share our Jesus story?

1. Know the Mission You Have.

They went out, going from town to town. They preached the Good News and healed the sick everywhere. Jesus said to them, "There is much grain ready to gather. But the workmen are few. Pray then to the Lord Who is the Owner of the grain-fields that He will send workmen to gather His grain.

➢ Be, Pray, Heal, and Preach the Good News

2. Know the power you have.

Jesus called His twelve followers to Him. He gave them the right and the power over all demons and to heal diseases. Vs. 9:1

³ Go on your way. Listen! I send you out like lambs among wolves.

They said, "Lord, even the demons obeyed us when we used Your name." Verse 10:17

- The Right
- The Power

3. Know the message you have.

² *He sent them to preach about the holy nation of God and to heal the sick.*

➢ The Kingdom of God, the Holy Nation of God.

4. **Know the method you have.**

² He sent them to preach about the holy nation of God and to heal the sick. "Take nothing along for the trip. Do not take a walking stick or a bag or bread or money. Do not take two coats! ⁴ Whatever house you go into, stay there until you are ready to go on. ⁵ If anyone will not take you in, as you leave that city, shake its dust off your feet. That will speak against them."

³ Go on your way. Listen! I send you out like lambs among wolves. ⁴ Take no money. Do not take a bag or shoes. Speak to no one along the way. ⁵ When you go into a house, say that you hope peace will come to them. ⁶ If a man who loves peace lives there, your good wishes will come to him. If your good wishes are not received, they will come back to you. ⁷ Stay in the same house. Eat and drink what they give you. The workman should have his thanks. Do not move from house to house. ⁸ "Whenever a city receives you, eat the things that are put before you there. ⁹ Heal the sick. Say to them, 'The holy nation of God is near.' —Luke 10:3-9.

➤ Take very little with you.
➤ Bless the home, Community, City, and Country
➤ Cultivate a relationship—make friends.
➤ Do Not ague or Fight with people.
➤ Help bring healing and health.
➤ Preach, proclaim, tell, declare, and speak about Jesus.

5. **Know the Meaning you have.**

They went out, going from town to town. They preached the Good News and healed the sick everywhere.

[17] The seventy came back full of joy. They said, "Lord, even the demons obeyed us when we used Your name." [18] Jesus said to them, "I saw Satan fall from heaven like lightning. [19] Listen! I have given you power to walk on snakes. I have given you power over small animals with a sting of poison. I have given you power over all the power of the one who works against you. Nothing will hurt you. [20] Even so, you should not be happy because the demons obey you but be happy because your names are written in heaven."

> ➤ **The Joy**
> ➤ **The Name in the book of Life**

CONCLUSION

We are all called to share our faith and play a part in the great commission. There are several ways in which we can do it. We do this by being salt and light, through the way we live our lives before others. We can verbally share the Gospel. We can share our story. We can invite others to church services, or other Christian gatherings.

We should always pray for the salvation of others, and make sure that we are motivated by love.

Small Group Lesson: A DISCIPLE SHARES THE FAITH IN LOVE

First of all, then, I urge that supplications, prayers, intercessions, and thanksgivings be made for all people, 2 for kings and all who are in high positions, that we may lead a peaceful and quiet life, godly and dignified in every way. 3 This is good, and it is pleasing in the sight of God our Savior, 4 who desires all people to be saved and to come to the knowledge of the truth.1.

~1 Tim 2:1-4

INTRODUCTION – "The greatest way we can show love to another person is by sharing the gospel of Jesus Christ to them. When a man is filled with the Word of God you cannot keep him still, If a man has got the Word, he must speak or die."
-Dwight L. Moody

TALK IT OVER

True Disciples know that...

1. Sharing the gospel is for Every Believer and is to All Nations. ~**Matt. 4:19**

2. The kingdom Needs More Workers. ~ **Matt 9:37**
3. Sharing our faith Requires Prayers and Absolute Dependence on God. ~ **Matt 9:38**

4. Sharing our faith Demands Living the story we share, and it may Bring us persecution. ~ **Matt 10:22**

5. Sharing our faith is Relationship Driven and Being a servant

Let us find out How to share our Jesus story in Love:

1. Know the Mission You Have ~ **Matt 28:19**

2. Know the power you have ~ **Luke 9:1, Luke 10:17**

3. Know the message you have ~ **Luke 9:2-4**

4. Know the method you have ~ **Luke 10:3-9**

5. Know the Meaning you have ~ **Luke 10:17-20**

DISCOVERY QUESTIONS

1. What motivated God to give His Son? Who did God give His Son for? What standing do people have before God if they do not believe in Jesus?

2. What does the Bible say about sharing our faith? what is the mission of the church according to Jesus?

PRAYER DIRECTION

1. Dear Lord, give our congregations a passion and a burden for souls and unreached people. - ***Rom. 9:1-3; 10:1***

2. Dear Lord, help our members see that their primary place of ministry is beyond the church walls. - ***Matt. 10:8***

13

LOVE IS GENEROUS (PART 1)— UNDERSTANDING MONEY AND WEALTH

"No one can serve two masters, for either he will hate the one and love the other, or he will be devoted to the one and despise the other. You cannot serve God and money.—Matthew 6:24 ESV

But seek first the kingdom of God and his righteousness, and all these things will be added to you.—Matthew 6:33 ESV

OUTLINE

- Questions
- Quotes
- Church And Money
- God And Money
- Laws of Money
- Wealth Creation Challenge

QUESTIONS

1. What is money?
2. What is wealth?
3. Does God want us to prosper and be wealthy?
4. Do we know how God want us to prosper and be very wealthy?

5. What are the practical ways to prosper and be wealthy?
6. What are the scriptural ways to prosper and be wealthy?
7. What is the Bible prescription for money?

8. How do we use money and wealth to partner with God to help others and impact nations?
9. Why does God want you wealthy?

QUOTES ABOUT MONEY

➢ Money is the representative of a certain quantity of corn or other commodity. It is so much warmth, so much bread. — *Ralph Waldo Emerson*
➢ Wouldst, thou shut up the avenues of ill, pay every debt as if God wrote the bill.
➢ Can anybody remember when the times were not hard and money not scarce?
➢ Men such as they are, very naturally seek money or power; and power because it is as good as money.
➢ Money is of no value; it cannot spend itself. All depends on the skill of the spender.
➢ A man is usually more careful of his money than he is of his principles.
➢ Without a rich heart, wealth is an ugly beggar.
➢ The whole value of the dime is in knowing what to do with it.
➢ It tells us what items cost, and what they are worth.
➢ Money represents what you are giving your life's energy to.
➢ Money is just the middleman. In reality, money prevents us from having to carry chickens and bushels of apples with us to

buy things. We have this freedom because money acts as the currency in the middle.

➢ No one will remember the Good Samaritan if he had good intentions only, he had money as well.—*Margaret Thatcher*
➢ I was put on earth to get rich, to collect the money that already had my name on it, and then give it all away.
➢ There is opportunity. God want us to make money in partnership with God. God's way, Gods will, for God's purpose.

MY STORY

What if?

➢ I Replace my salary + benefits with passive income?
➢ I was a minister with real estate investments?
➢ I have a system that is making money for me, so I do not have to be taking money from the church?
➢ How do I do it? And what are the right reasons?
➢ It is not about what I have but what I can give. It is about the impact that I can make in the Kingdom of God.
➢ How do we become financially free? What would that mean to you? To your family? And to the church?
➢ How do we build wealth in the kingdom context?
➢ How do the wealthy build their wealth?

Note: When it comes to money and wealth, God is no respecter of persons.

CHURCH AND MONEY

Most people are taught in Canada and the church on how to "earn" and "save" money, but most people are not taught how to "make", "create money" or "live off of" their money.

Few or not many people ask the question. How do you make the money work for you? How do I make sense of making money to make a difference in the world?

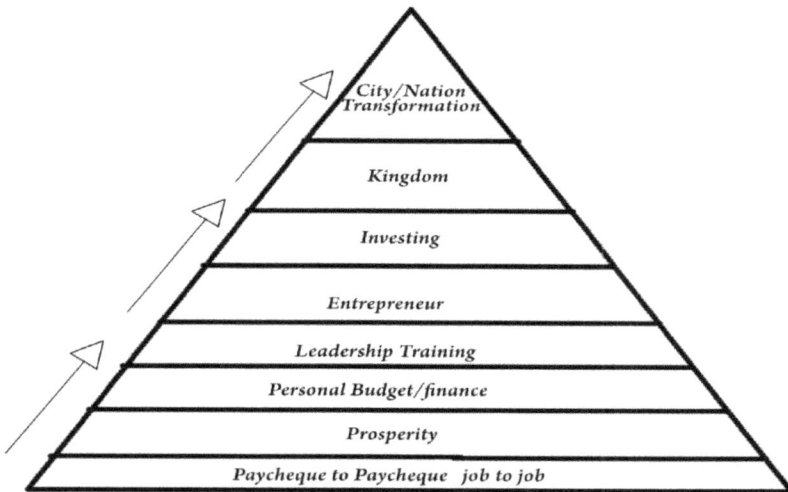

GOD AND MONEY

And my God shall supply all your need according to His riches in glory by Christ Jesus. —Philippians 4:19

I will give you hidden treasures, riches stored in secret places, so that you may know that I am the LORD, the God of Israel, who summons you by name. —Isaiah 45:3

16 And he told them this parable: "The ground of a certain rich man yielded an abundant harvest. 17 He thought to himself, 'What shall I do? I have no place to store my crops.' 18 "Then he said, 'This is what I'll do. I will tear down my barns and build bigger ones, and there I will store my surplus grain. 19 And I'll say to myself, "You have plenty of grain laid up for many years. Take life easy; eat, drink and be merry."' 20 "But God said to him, 'You fool! This very night your life will be demanded from you. Then who will get what you have prepared for yourself?' 21 "This is how it will be with whoever stores up things for themselves but is not rich toward God." —Luke 12:16-21

17 You may say to yourself, "My power and the strength of my hands have produced this wealth for me." 18 But remember the LORD your God, for it is he who gives you the ability to produce wealth, and so confirms his covenant, which he swore to your ancestors, as it is today. —Deuteronomy 8: 17-18 AMP

10 For the love of money is a root of all kinds of evil. Some people, eager for money, have wandered from the faith and pierced themselves with many griefs. —1 Timothy 6:10

Note: A person can be broke, and love money, this has to do with the attitude of your heart.

4 "No one can serve two masters, for either he will hate[a] the one and love the other, or he will be devoted to the one and despise the other. You cannot serve God and money.—Matthew 6:24

Note: We are in partnership with God in establishing his kingdom on earth.

Thy kingdom come; thy will be done on earth as it is in heaven. We are partners together with God to accomplish and advance His kingdom on earth.

THE 5 LAWS OF MONEY AND WEALTH

1. The Law of Connection
2. The Law of Stewardship
3. The Law of Wisdom
4. The Law of Risk
5. The Law of Investment

Matthew 25:14-30 Message Bible.

14-18 "It's also like a man going off on an extended trip. He called his servants together and delegated responsibilities. To one he gave five thousand dollars, to another two thousand, to a third one thousand, depending on their abilities. Then he left. Right off, the first servant went to work and doubled his master's investment. The second did the same. But the man with the single thousand dug a hole and carefully buried his master's money. 19-21 "After a long absence, the master of those three servants came back and settled up with them. The one given five thousand dollars showed him how he had doubled his investment. His master commended him: 'Good work! You did your job well. From now on be my partner.'

22-23 "The servant with the two thousand showed how he also had doubled his master's investment. His master commended him: 'Good work! You did your job well. From now on be my partner.' 24-25 "The servant given one thousand said, 'Master, I know you have high standards and hate careless ways, that you demand the best and make no allowances for error. I was afraid I might disappoint you, so I found a good hiding place and secured your money. Here it is, safe and sound down to the last cent.' 26-27 "The master was furious. 'That's a terrible way to live! It's criminal to live cautiously like that! If you knew I was after the best, why did you do less than the least? The least you could have done would have been to invest the sum with the bankers, where at least I would have gotten a little interest. 28-30 "'Take the thousand and give it to the one who risked the most. And get rid of this "play-it-safe" who won't go out on a limb. Throw him out into utter darkness.'

1. The Law of Connection
2. The Law of Stewardship
3. The law of Wisdom—
   Through [skillful and godly] wisdom a house [a life, a home, a family] is built, And by understanding it is established [on a sound and good foundation], 4 And by knowledge its rooms are filled, With all precious and pleasant riches.—Proverbs 24:3-4 AMP
4. The Law of Risk
5. The Law of Investments.

Note: How many of us are able to take one dollar and turn it into two dollars? How is wealth created?

Wealth is created when assets move from lower to higher-valued assets. —Managerial Economics

WEALTH CREATING CHALLENGE

- Become a steward. Luke 16:10
- Develop a budget. Proverb 27:23-24
- Become debt-free. Proverbs 10:22; 22:7
- Become generous. Give at least a Tithe. Proverbs 3:9

Reference:

"Money Mastery"—Making sense of making money to make a difference in the Kingdom of God. Book by Billy Epperhart

Small Group Lesson: UNDERSTANDING MONEY & WEALTH

24No man can serve two masters: for either he will hate the one, and love the other; or else he will hold to the one, and despise the other. Ye cannot serve God and mammon. 33But seek ye first the kingdom of God, and his righteousness; and all these things shall be added unto you.
~Matt 6:24 & 33

INTRODUCTION – Most people are taught in Canada and the church on how to "earn" and "save" money, but most people are not taught how to "make", "create money" or "live off" of their money.
A Few or not many people ask the question. How do you make the money work for you? How do I make sense of making money to make a difference in the world? God want us to make money in partnership with God. God's way, Gods will, for God's purpose.

LET'S DISCUSS THESE QUESTIONS

1. **What is the difference between money and wealth?**

2. **Does God want us to prosper and be wealthy?**
   Beloved, I pray that in every way you may prosper and enjoy good health, as your soul also prospers. ~ *3 John 1:2*

3. Do we know how God want us to prosper and be very wealthy?

   I will give you hidden treasures, riches stored in secret places, so that you may know that I am the LORD, the God of Israel, who summons you by name. **~ Isaiah 45:3**

4. What are the practical ways to prosper and be wealthy?

5. What is the Bible prescriptions for money?

   But seek ye first the kingdom of God, and his righteousness; and all these things shall be added unto you. **~Matt 6:33**

6. How do we use money and wealth to partner with God to help others and impact nations?

7. Why does God want you wealthy?

   You may say to yourself, "My power and the strength of my hands have produced this wealth for me." 18 But remember the LORD your God, for it is he who gives you the ability to produce wealth, **and so confirms his covenant, which he swore to your ancestors, as it is today.** **~Deuteronomy 8:17-18**

WEALTH CREATING CHALLENGE

- Become a Steward. *~Luke 16:10*
- Develop a budget. *~Proverb 27:23-24*
- Become debt Free. *~Proverbs 10:22; 22:7*
- Be Generous, Give at least a Tithe. *~Proverbs 3:9*

PRAYER DIRECTION

1. Heavenly Father, I stand upon Proverbs 13:22 that states "a good man leaves an inheritance for his children's children, but a sinner's wealth is stored up for the righteous." Father, I am believing in you for creative ideas and opportunities to build wealth in order to leave a legacy for my children's children. Let this be done according to your will.

2. Lord Jesus, anoint my eyes to see the hidden riches of this world and bless me with them and make me a financial pillar in your church.

14

LOVE IS GENEROUS (PART 2)— UNDERSTANDING MONEY AND WEALTH

⁷ "And when you pray, do not heap up empty phrases as the Gentiles do, for they think that they will be heard for their many words. ⁸ Do not be like them, for your Father knows what you need before you ask him. ⁹ Pray then like this: "Our Father in heaven, hallowed be your name. ¹⁰ Your kingdom come, your will be done, on earth as it is in heaven. ¹¹ Give us this day our daily bread, ¹² and forgive us our debts, as we also have forgiven our debtors. ¹³ And lead us not into temptation, but deliver us from evil. ¹⁴ For if you forgive others their trespasses, your heavenly Father will also forgive you,

—Matthew 6:5-14 ESV

OUTLINE:

1. Questions about money
2. Church and money
3. Jews and money
4. Paul and money
5. Jesus and money

PURPOSE:

To encourage us to know that God wants His children blessed in wisdom, health, and wealth so we can build His Kingdom on earth as it is in heaven.

IMAGINATIVE QUESTIONS

1. What is your financial situation now?
2. Do you believe that God wants you to be rich, wealthy, and healthy?
3. What is money to you as a child of God?
4. Do you know how to earn money?
5. Do you know how to make money work for you?
6. Do you know how to make money work without you?
7. Do you believe that God needs businessmen and women?
8. How will it feel like to be financially free? No credit card debt, no car loans, no mortgages, no student loan?
9. What difference can you make in your life, family, church, country, and community if you are financially free?
10. What about the church? Living Word Assembly of God. What about all churches?

CHURCH AND MONEY

Most people are taught in Canada and the church on how to "earn" and "save" money, but most people are not taught how to "make", "create money" or "live off of" their money.

Four questions about money we should always be asking:

- How do you earn money?
- How do you make money work for you?
- How do you make money work without you?
- How do I make sense of making money to make a difference in the world?

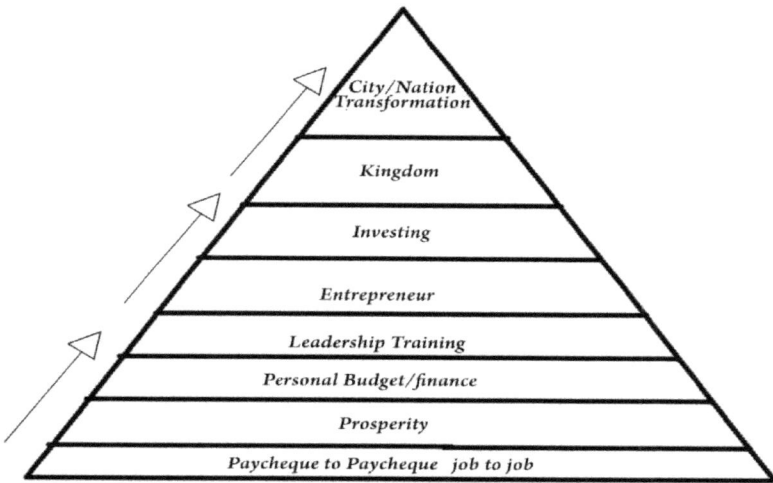

In 1975, Bill Bright, founder of Campus Crusade and Loren Cunningham, founder of Youth with a Mission (YWAM), developed a God-given, world-changing strategy. Their mandate: Bring Godly change to a nation by reaching its seven spheres, or mountains, of societal influence. They concluded that in order to truly transform any nation with the Gospel of Jesus Christ, these seven facets of society must be reached: Religion, Family,

Education, Government, Media, Arts & Entertainment and Business.[8]

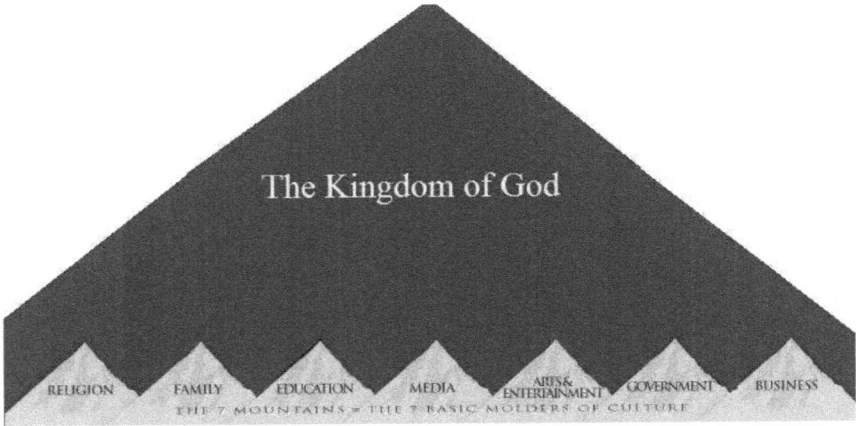

THE JEWS AND MONEY

[17] Beware lest you say in your heart, 'My power and the might of my hand have gotten me this wealth.' [18] You shall remember the LORD your God, for it is he who gives you power to get wealth, that he may confirm his covenant that he swore to your fathers, as it is this day.
—Deuteronomy 8:17-18

In the article *"Judaism, Markets and Capitalism: separating myths from Reality,"* Corrine and Robert M. Sauer clarify the Jewish Economics Theory or concept of riches and wealth in **six foundations** based on the Old Testament:

---

[8] https://www.generals.org/the-seven-mountains

What is the Jewish mindset and view of money?

As Christians most of us take a fearful approach to riches and wealth. Perhaps, we can learn from the Jewish mindset:

1. Participation in the creative process

In the New Testament, the Apostle Paul tells us in 2 Corinthians 6:1 that we are co-laborers together with God. God has His part to play, and we have our part to play. God's part is grace, while our part is faith. God gives Adam a Garden and tells him to cultivate it. God promises Israel a land and expect them to go and possess it.

2. Protection of private property

This foundation says that it is important to have property or, in other words, to become an **owner**. The idea here is that, when you own something, you have the opportunity to become a steward of that which you own.

3. The accumulation of wealth as virtue

In Jewish Economic theory, they believe that accumulating of wealth is a good thing and a godly thing. The Jewish mindset sees being able to steward and mange wealth as being "holy in the earth" but in the western mindset, most people do not see it that way.

4. Caring for the needy

This was a command God gave his children. Caring for the needy. Always give aid in times of crisis. How can you give if you do not have? But always remember this cliché when it comes to charity: Instead of giving somebody a fish so they can eat the fish, teach them how to fish. This way, they will always have food to eat. Make the needy and poor, self sufficient.

5. Limited Government

This has to do with governments and the tax structure than anything. The Jews believe there should be government, but it should be limited to allow people freedom to live and engage in enterprise.

6. Work is worship. -"Tikkun Olam"

The sixth Jewish mindset is that they consider work to be the same as worship. There is an understanding of a marketplace, kingdom sound in the earth. God has bigger plans and bigger purpose. He wants to see His people empowered so that we can see His kingdom come to earth as it is in heaven.

Source: *"Money Mastery"—Making sense of making money to make a difference in the Kingdom of God.* Book by Billy Epperhart

PAUL ON MONEY

1 Timothy 6:17-18 passage reads:

"Command those who are rich in this present world not to be arrogant nor to put their hope in wealth, which is so uncertain, but to put their hope in God, who richly provides us with everything for our enjoyment. Command them to do good, to be rich in good deeds, and to be generous and willing to share."

When your season of money and material wealth arrives, if it has not already, Paul, the Apostle in 1 Timothy 6:17-18 passage is telling us to do the following four things:

1. Do not become arrogant.

Work hard and become successful in life but do not think of yourself as better than others because of your material wealth. In Deuteronomy 8:18 Moses reminds us, *"But remember the Lord your God, for it is he who gives you the ability to produce wealth."*

2. Do not put your hope in your wealth.

Proverbs 23:5 says, *"Cast but a glance at riches, and they are gone, for they will surely sprout wings and fly off to the sky like an eagle."* A good job or business and its steady earnings can be here today and gone tomorrow.

3. Be rich in good deeds.

A good deed is a free and voluntary act of service toward another person. Doing good deeds for others is the fruit of your salvation in Jesus Christ. Ephesians 2:10 tells us: *"For we are God's workmanship, created in Christ Jesus to do good works."*

4. Be generous and willing to share.

Generous people are **synergistic**. They build organizations and contribute to the success of others. Think about it: who wants to do business with someone who only takes?

JESUS AND MONEY

Matthew 13:

3 He told many stories in the form of parables, such as this one: "Listen! A farmer went out to plant some seeds. 24 Here is another story Jesus told: "The Kingdom of Heaven is like a farmer who planted good seed in his field. 31 Here is another illustration Jesus used: "The Kingdom of Heaven is like a mustard seed planted in a field. 32 It is the smallest of all seeds, but it becomes the largest of garden plants; it grows into a tree, and birds come and make nests in its branches." 33 Jesus also used this illustration: "The Kingdom of Heaven is like the yeast a woman used in making bread. Even though she put only a little yeast in three measures of flour, it permeated every part of the dough." 44 "The Kingdom of Heaven is like a treasure that a man discovered hidden in a field. In his excitement, he hid it again and sold everything he owned to get enough money to buy the field. ⁴⁵ *"Again, the Kingdom of Heaven is like a merchant on the lookout for choice pearls.* ⁴⁶ *When he discovered a pearl of great value, he sold everything he owned and bought it!* ⁴⁷ *"Again, the Kingdom of Heaven is like a fishing net that was thrown into the water and caught fish of every kind.*

Luke 10:30-35

³⁰ *Jesus replied with a story: "A Jewish man was traveling from Jerusalem down to Jericho, and he was attacked by bandits. They stripped him of his clothes, beat him up, and left him half dead beside the road.* ³¹ *"By chance a priest came along. But when he saw the man lying there, he crossed to the other side of the road and passed him by.* ³² *A Temple assistant^[a] walked over and looked at him lying there, but he also passed by on the other side.* ³³ *"Then a despised Samaritan came along, and when he saw the man, he felt compassion for him.* ³⁴ *Going over to him, the Samaritan soothed his wounds with olive oil and wine and bandaged them. Then he put the man on his own donkey and took him to an inn, where he took care of him.* ³⁵ *The next day he handed the innkeeper two silver coins,^[b] telling him, 'Take care of this man. If his bill runs higher than this, I'll pay you the next time I'm here.'*

Why didn't the priest and the temple assistant help the guy out?

CONCLUSION

I believe that God want us, as members of Living Word to be blessed, by following the understanding of money as revealed by the Jews, in the Old Testament, Paul and Jesus.

He wants us, as His church, to build wealth. God wants us to have some barns. But it is not necessarily about building bigger barns. It is about us prospering in the barns we already have.

When it comes time to building bigger barns, that is when we begin to partner with God in the process of "tikkun Olam", to bring the mundane up to the holy. This is God's purpose for wealth and riches.

15

LOVE IS GENEROUS (PART 3)— UNDERSTANDING MONEY AND WEALTH: THE ABRAHAMIC PRINCIPLES

QUOTES

"We all have two choices: We can make a living, or we can design a life."— Jim Rohn

"Formal education will make you a living; self-education will make you a fortune."—Jim Rohn.

RECAP:

Six Foundations for wealth and money

1. Participation in the creative process
2. Protection of private property
3. Accumulation of wealth as virtue
4. Caring for the needy
5. Limited Government
6. Work Is Worship

PURPOSE:

Encourage ourselves to know that when we live our lives by following the example of our father Abraham we will be blessed by God.

QUESTIONS

1. What are some of the things that you think are more important than money?

Answers: Time, desperation, desire, determination, courage, ambition, faith, ingenuity, heart and soul, personality, relationships, health,

2. How do people become wealthy? What are some of the ways to become wealthy?

Answer: (Invest in You) Add value to you, get a job, stay out of debt, build a business, invest in real estate, in stocks, royalties, the Kingdom, other people.

3. How did our Father Abraham create his wealth?
4. How do we become wealthy like our Father Abraham?

Answers: The Abrahamic Example—Practices and Principles

The Call of Abram

12 Now the LORD said to Abram, "Go from your country and your kindred and your father's house to the land that I will show you. 2 And I will make of you a great nation, and I will bless you and make your name great, so that you will be a blessing. 3 I will bless those who bless you, and him who dishonors you I will curse, and in you all the families of the earth shall be blessed."

4 So Abram went, as the LORD had told him, and Lot went with him. Abram was seventy-five years old when he departed from Haran. 5 And Abram took Sarai his wife, and Lot his brother's son, and all their possessions that they had gathered, and the people that they had acquired in Haran, and they set out to go to the land of Canaan. When they came to the land of Canaan, 6 Abram passed through the land to the place at Shechem, to the oak of Moreh. At that time the Canaanites were in the land. 7 Then the LORD appeared to Abram and said, "To your offspring I will give this land." So he built there an altar to the LORD, who had appeared to him. 8 From there he moved to the hill country on the east of Bethel and pitched his tent, with Bethel on the west and Ai on the east. And there he built an altar to the LORD and called upon the name of the LORD. 9 And Abram journeyed on, still going toward the Negeb.

1. Obey the voice and leading of God.
2. Know what you have.
3. Build God an Alter and Call on His name.

Abram and Sarai in Egypt

10 Now there was a famine in the land. So, Abram went down to Egypt to sojourn there, for the famine was severe in the land. 11 When he was about to enter Egypt, he said to Sarai his wife, "I know that you are a woman beautiful in appearance, 12 and when the Egyptians see you, they will say, 'This is his wife.' Then they will kill me, but they will let you live. 13 Say you are my sister, that it may go well with me because of you, and that my life may be spared for your sake." 14 When Abram entered Egypt, the Egyptians saw that the woman was very beautiful. 15 And when the princes of Pharaoh saw her, they praised her to Pharaoh. And the woman was taken into Pharaoh's house. 16 And for her sake he dealt well with Abram; and he had sheep, oxen, male donkeys, male servants, female servants, female donkeys, and camels.

17 But the L*ORD afflicted Pharaoh and his house with great plagues because of Sarai, Abram's wife. 18 So Pharaoh called Abram and said, "What is this you have done to me? Why did you not tell me that she was your wife? 19 Why did you say, 'She is my sister,' so that I took her for my wife? Now then, here is your wife; take her, and go." 20 And Pharaoh gave men orders concerning him, and they sent him away with his wife and all that he had.*

4. Face the famine without compromise.
5. Build a business based on your gift and passion.

Abram and Lot Separate

13 So Abram went up from Egypt, he, and his wife and all that he had, and Lot with him, into the Negeb.

2 Now Abram was very rich in livestock, in silver, and in gold. 3 And he journeyed on from the Negeb as far as Bethel to the place where his tent had been at the beginning, between Bethel and Ai, 4 to the place where he had made an altar at the first. And there Abram called upon the name of the L*ORD. 5 And Lot, who went with Abram, also had flocks and herds and tents, 6 so that the land could not support both of them dwelling together; for their possessions were so great that they could not dwell together, 7 and there was strife between the herdsmen of Abram's livestock and the herdsmen of Lot's livestock. At that time the Canaanites and the Perizzites were dwelling in the land.*

8 Then Abram said to Lot, "Let there be no strife between you and me, and between your herdsmen and my herdsmen, for we are kinsmen. 9 Is not the whole land before you? Separate yourself from me. If you take the left hand, then I will go to the right, or if you take the right hand, then I will go to the left." **10** *And Lot lifted up his eyes and saw that the Jordan Valley was well watered everywhere like the garden of the* LORD, *like the land of Egypt, in the direction of Zoar. (This was before the* LORD *destroyed Sodom and Gomorrah.)* **11** *So Lot chose for himself all the Jordan Valley, and Lot journeyed east. Thus, they separated from each other.* **12** *Abram settled in the land of Canaan, while Lot settled among the cities of the valley and moved his tent as far as Sodom.* **13** *Now the men of Sodom* ⁿ*were wicked, great sinners against the* LORD.

14 *The* LORD *said to Abram, after Lot had separated from him, "Lift up your eyes and look from the place where you are,* ᵒ*northward and southward and eastward and westward,* **15** *for all the land that you see I will give to you and to your offspring forever.* **16** *I will make your offspring as the dust of the earth, so that if one can count the dust of the earth, your offspring also can be counted.* **17** *Arise, walk through the length and the breadth of the land, for I will give it to you."* **18** *So Abram moved his tent and came and settled by the oaks of Mamre, which are at Hebron, and there he built an altar to the* LORD.

6. Invest in livestock, Gold and Silver.
7. Pursue peace, not conflict and quarrels.
8. Continue to Obey the voice and leading of God.

Note: Like Abraham we should not take a fearful approach to wealth.

CONCLUSION

The Abrahamic principles for understanding money and wealth:

1. Obey the voice and leading of God.
2. Know what you have.
3. Build God an Alter and Call on His name.
4. Face the famine without compromise.
5. Build a business based on your gifts.
6. Invest in livestock, Gold and Silver.
7. Pursue peace, not conflict and quarrels.
8. Obey the voice and leading of God.

Small Group Lesson: UNDERSTANDING MONEY AND WEALTH—THE ABRAHAMIC PRINCIPLES

Scripture Reading: ~ **Gen 12:1-20 and Gen 13:1-18**

INTRODUCTION – The real measure of your wealth is how much you'd be worth if you lost all your money. Poor people spend their money and save what's left, rich people save their money and spend what's left. We all have two choices: We can make a living, or we can design a life. Formal education will make you a living; self-education will make you a fortune.
~ Jim Rohn

LET'S DISCUSS THESE QUESTIONS

1. **What are some of the things that you think are more important than money?** (Hints: Time, Relationship, Faith)

   How much better it is to get wisdom than gold! And to get understanding is to be chosen above silver.
      ~ **Prov 16:16** (AMP)

2. **What was God's command and promise to Abraham, and what was Abraham's response, that led to his blessings?**

   The Lord had said to Abram, Go from your country, your people and your father's household to the land I will show you. I will make you into a great nation, and I will bless you; I will make

your name great, and you will be a blessing I will bless those who bless you, and whoever curses you I will curse; and all peoples on earth will be blessed through you. ~
Gen 12:1-3

3. Why was Abraham's decision to build an alter to the Lord important and what can we learn from him?
   Read this Verse ~ *Gen12:6-9*

4. How did Abraham build his wealth and what can we learn or apply from his example to our lives?

   So Abram went up from Egypt to the Negev, with his wife and everything he had, and Lot went with him. 2 Abram had become very wealthy in livestock and in silver and gold. 3 From the Negev he went from place to place until he came to Bethel, to the place between Bethel and Ai where his tent had been earlier ~ *Gen 13:1-3*

PRAYER DIRECTION

1. Dear Lord, I pray that from now on all my investments and labour since the beginning of my career and ministry will begin to yield their full profit in Jesus' name.

2. Oh Lord, baptize me with the generous spirit of a cheerful giver who gives out of love and not out of compulsion.

3. Lord Jesus, just as the famine led Abraham to Egypt and was eventually blessed, help me Lord to see the opportunity that the current pandemic is creating for my prosperity in Jesus' name.

16

LOVE IS GRATEFUL (PART 1)— UNDERSTANDING THE IMPORTANCE OF GRATITUDE

⁴ Enter his gates with thanksgiving and his courts with praise; give thanks to him and praise his name. Let us come before him with thanksgiving and extol him with music and song.—Psalm 100:4

TEXT:

PSALM 100:4; 95:2; 107:1-43

PURPOSE

To challenge and encourage us to know how important it is to be grateful, so we can stay grateful to the end.

QUESTION

Do you believe that "As you are right now, you have something to thank God for?"

The Psalmist shows us 7 kinds of people.

1. The Lonely

2. The Stuck
3. The Sick
4. The Needy
5. The Prisoner
6. The Broke
7. The Storm

PSALM 107

Verses 1-7

¹ Give thanks to the Lord, for he is good; his love endures forever. ² Let the redeemed of the Lord tell their story— those he redeemed from the hand of the foe, ³ those he gathered from the lands, from east and west, from north and south. ⁴ Some wandered in desert wastelands, finding no way to a city where they could settle. ⁵ They were hungry and thirsty, and their lives ebbed away. ⁶ Then they cried out to the Lord in their trouble, and he delivered them from their distress. ⁷ He led them by a straight way to a city where they could settle.

1. Principles

➢ Gratitude focuses on God's Goodness and unfailing love.
➢ Gratitude focuses on God's redemption and deliverance.
➢ Gratitude tells the redemption story.

Verses 8-14

⁸ Let them give thanks to the Lord for his unfailing love and his wonderful deeds for mankind, ⁹ for he satisfies the thirsty and fills the hungry with good things. *¹⁰Some sat in darkness, in utter darkness, prisoners suffering in iron chains, ¹¹ because they rebelled against God's commands and despised the plans of the Most High. ¹² So he subjected them to bitter labor; they stumbled, and there was no one to help. ¹³* **Then they cried to the Lord in their trouble, and he saved them from their distress.** *¹⁴ He brought them out of darkness, the utter darkness, and broke away their chains.*

2. Principles

- ➢ Gratitude focuses on God's wonderful works.
- ➢ Gratitude focuses on God's provision—The thirsty, hungry, rebellion, and the distressed.

Verses 15-20

¹⁵ Let them give thanks to the Lord for his unfailing love and his wonderful deeds for mankind, ¹⁶ for he breaks down gates of bronze and cuts through bars of iron.

¹⁷ Some became fools through their rebellious ways and suffered affliction because of their iniquities. ¹⁸ They loathed all food and drew near the gates of death. ¹⁹ Then they cried to the Lord in their trouble, and he saved them from their distress. ²⁰ He sent out his word and healed them; he rescued them from the grave.

3. Principles

- ➢ Gratitude focuses on God's divine healing.

> Gratitude focuses on the impossible made possible.
> Gratitude focuses on God's protection from death and the grave.

Verses 21-30

²¹ Let them give thanks to the Lord for his unfailing love and his wonderful deeds for mankind. ²² Let them sacrifice thank offerings and tell of his works with songs of joy. ²³ Some went out on the sea in ships; they were merchants on the mighty waters. ²⁴ They saw the works of the Lord, his wonderful deeds in the deep. ²⁵ For he spoke and stirred up a tempest that lifted high the waves. ²⁶ They mounted up to the heavens and went down to the depths; in their peril their courage melted away. ²⁷ They reeled and staggered like drunkards; they were at their wits' end. ²⁸ Then they cried out to the Lord in their trouble, and he brought them out of their distress. ²⁹ He stilled the storm to a whisper; the waves of the sea were hushed. ³⁰ They were glad when it grew calm, and he guided them to their desired haven.

4. Principles

> Gratitude focuses on been generous to God.
> Gratitude focuses on sacrificing a thanks offering.
> Gratitude focuses on offering songs of joy.

Verses 31-43

³¹ Let them give thanks to the Lord for his unfailing love and his wonderful deeds for mankind. ³² Let them exalt him in the assembly of the people and praise him in the council of the elders. ³³ He turned rivers into a desert, flowing springs into thirsty ground, ³⁴ and fruitful land into a salt waste, because of the wickedness of those who lived there. ³⁵ He turned the desert into pools of water and the parched ground into flowing springs; ³⁶ there he brought the hungry to live, and they founded a city where they could settle. ³⁷ They sowed fields and planted vineyards that yielded a fruitful harvest; ³⁸ he blessed them, and their numbers greatly increased, and he did not let their herds diminish. ³⁹ Then their numbers decreased, and they were humbled by oppression, calamity, and sorrow; ⁴⁰ he who pours contempt on nobles made them wander in a trackless waste. ⁴¹ But he lifted the needy out of their affliction and increased their families like flocks. ⁴² The upright see and rejoice, but all the wicked shut their mouths. ⁴³ Let the one who is wise heed these things and ponder the loving deeds of the Lord.

5. Principles

➢ Gratitude focuses on public worship of God.
➢ Gratitude Focuses on remaining wise.
➢ Gratitude focuses on meditating on the loving deeds of God.

PRAYER

I am considering your great love for me today, Lord, and admit it is over my heard. You heard my cry when I was lonely, trapped, sick, broke, in need and in a storm. My unworthiness did not stop You for a moment. You, touched untouchables, also took firm hold on me and I thank you.

Small Group Lesson: UNDERSTANDING THE IMPORTANCE OF GRATITUDE

Enter his gates with thanksgiving and his courts with praise; give thanks to him and praise his name. Let us come before him with thanksgiving and extol him with music and song.

~ Psalm 100:4

INTRODUCTION – Gratitude is what we experience when we perceive that what we have received is an undeserved gift of God's grace. It is a fruit of humility; it's inherently unselfish. We don't feel true gratitude toward ourselves, but only towards someone else who treats us better than we deserve. Thankful people are not only the most spiritually healthy and spiritually protected, but very often the happiest.

This week we will look at the gratitude of King David in 1 Chronicles 16. David's thankfulness was an expression and overflow of his worship.

Read 1 Chronicles 15:1-3, 15:25-29 &1 Chronicles 16:7-36

DISCOVERY QUESTIONS

1. What are some things you notice from this passage about gratefulness? What is the context in which this is taking place?

2. How does thankfulness affect your life and the lives of others?   Where does thankfulness/gratitude come from?

3. Why did David assemble all of Israel in Jerusalem, then they brought in the Ark? (**1 Chron. 1-3**)

4. In **1 Chron. 15:27-29**, why is David dancing and singing in the streets and why was Saul's daughter so angry and despised King David?

5. In **1 Chronicles 16:7-36**, what are some of the words that stick out to you that David used in his psalm of thanksgiving and why did David choose these words (Note: it was a celebration, a time of remembrance, and a time of praise, because of God's goodness)

6. How does this passage give you encouragement? What is God teaching you through this story of how David expressed gratitude because the ark had it's home?

7. How does reading and applying what happened in **1 Chronicles 15-&16** help you develop a thankful heart?

8. Think about what Christ did for you on the cross, how should this create an attitude of thankfulness in you?

9. What causes you to not be thankful? How does pride stand in the way of your thankfulness? Is being thankful difficult for you?

RESPOND IN PRAYER

Next Steps
1. Share one small "next step of gratitude" that you feel God is calling you to take in the next 7 days.
2. Pray that God would open your eyes so that you can see how to be thankful.
3. Write down a prayer of thanksgiving this week.
4. Share with the group ways you can show gratitude this week? Look for those opportunities. Share them at the next meeting.

17

LOVE IS GRATEFUL (PART 2)—UNDERSTANDING THE IMPORTANCE OF GRATITUDE: THE JESUS EXAMPLE

If you can be grateful to God for where you came from and for where you are, no devil can stop you from seeing your God-given dreams come to pass! If you can be grateful, no devil can stop your destiny! If you can be grateful, nothing can prevent you from seeing your God.

[14] Make thankfulness your sacrifice to God, and keep the vows you made to the Most High. [15] Then call on me when you are in trouble, and I will rescue you, and you will give me glory."—Psalm 50:14-15

OUTLINE

1. Facts about Gratitude
2. Examples of Jesus
3. Practice of Gratitude.

FACTS ABOUT GRATITUDE

1. Gratitude is the confidence of access into God's Presence. Our time in God's Presence is only useful, helpful, significant, and beneficial if we went there with gratitude.

2. The prosperity and efficiency of our time in God's Presence is guaranteed by gratitude. Time in God's Presence is a waste without the sense of gratitude

3. Gratitude is a spiritual exercise and discipline that is filled with blessings of God.

4. Gratitude prepares the ground for answered prayer, especially in times of difficulty (Ps. 50:14-15; Lam. 3:22-23).

5. Gratitude in times of peace prepares the ground for answers in times of trouble:
   a. Only the heart of the grateful secures response from God in times of trouble
   b. The ungrateful will not experience divine help and answers to prayer.
   c. Until God is appreciated for what He did for you in the past, He is not fascinated in what you want Him to do for you in the present and the future.

Without gratitude you are excused from God and without God, you are on your own!

JESUS' EXAMPLE ON GRATITUDE

1. Thanking the father: "because thou hast hid these things from the wise and prudent, and hast revealed them unto babes" (Mt 11:25).
2. Saying this same phrase again with thanks in (Lk 10:21).
3. Before feeding the 4000 (Mt 15:36; Mk 8:6).
4. Before feeding the 5000 (Jn 6:11).
5. Before raising Lazarus from the dead (Jn 11:41).
6. Before sharing wine at the Passover meal (Lk 22:17-18).
7. Before breaking bread (Lk 22:19), and sharing wine (Mt 26:27; Mk 14:23) at The Last Supper.

EXAMPLE 1

1. **Thanking the Father:** *"because thou hast hid these things from the wise and prudent, and hast revealed them unto babes"* **(Mt 11:25).**

[20] Then Jesus began to denounce the towns where he had done so many of his miracles, because they had not repented of their sins and turned to God. [21] "What sorrow awaits you, Korazin and Bethsaida! For if the miracles I did in you had been done in wicked Tyre and Sidon, their people would have repented of their sins long ago, clothing themselves in burlap and throwing ashes on their heads to show their remorse. [22] I tell you, Tyre and Sidon will be better off on judgment day than you. [23] "And you people of Capernaum, will you be honored in heaven? No, you will go down to the place of the dead.[g] For if the miracles I did for you had been done in wicked Sodom, it would still

be here today. ²⁴ I tell you, even Sodom will be better off on judgment day than you." ²⁵ **At that time Jesus prayed this prayer: "O Father, Lord of heaven and earth, thank you for hiding these things from those who think themselves wise and clever, and for revealing them to the childlike.** *²⁶ Yes, Father, it pleased you to do it this way! ²⁷ "My Father has entrusted everything to me. No one truly knows the Son except the Father, and no one truly knows the Father except the Son and those to whom the Son chooses to reveal him." ²⁸ Then Jesus said, "Come to me, all of you who are weary and carry heavy burdens, and I will give you rest. ²⁹ Take my yoke upon you. Let me teach you, because I am humble and gentle at heart, and you will find rest for your souls. ³⁰ For my yoke is easy to bear, and the burden I give you is light."*

2. Saying this same phrase again with thanks in (Lk 10:21).

²¹ At that same time Jesus was filled with the joy of the Holy Spirit, and he said, "O Father, Lord of heaven and earth, **thank you for** *hiding these things from those who think themselves wise and clever, and for revealing them to the childlike. Yes, Father, it pleased you to do it this way. ²² "My Father has entrusted everything to me. No one truly knows the Son except the Father, and no one truly knows the Father except the Son and those to whom the Son chooses to reveal him." ²³ Then when they were alone, he turned to the disciples and said, "Blessed are the eyes that see what you have seen. ²⁴ I tell you, many prophets and kings longed to see what you see, but they did not see it. And they longed to hear what you hear, but they didn't hear it."*

PRACTICES:

1. Be Grateful to God for knowing Jesus as your Lord and Saviour.
2. Be Grateful for the ability to repent and turn to God.
3. Be Grateful for the honour you will receive in heaven.

EXAMPLE 2

3. Before feeding the 4000 (Mt 15:32-36; Mark 8:1-9)

³² Then Jesus called his disciples and told them, "I feel sorry for these people. They have been here with me for three days, and they have nothing left to eat. I don't want to send them away hungry, or they will faint along the way." ³³ The disciples replied, "Where would we get enough food here in the wilderness for such a huge crowd?" ³⁴ Jesus asked, "How much bread do you have?" They replied, "Seven loaves, and a few small fish." ³⁵ So Jesus told all the people to sit down on the ground. ³⁶ Then he took the seven loaves and the fish, thanked God for them, and broke them into pieces. He gave them to the disciples, who distributed the food to the crowd. ³⁷ They all ate as much as they wanted. Afterward, the disciples picked up seven large baskets of leftover food. ³⁸ There were 4,000 men who were fed that day, in addition to all the women and children. ³⁹ Then Jesus sent the people home, and he got into a boat and crossed over to the region of Magadan.

4. Before feeding the 5000 (John 6:1-15).

*After this, Jesus crossed over to the far side of the Sea of Galilee, also known as the Sea of Tiberias. ² A huge crowd kept following him wherever he went, because they saw his miraculous signs as he healed the sick. ³ Then Jesus climbed a hill and sat down with his disciples around him. ⁴ (It was nearly time for the Jewish Passover celebration.) ⁵ Jesus soon saw a huge crowd of people coming to look for him. Turning to Philip, he asked, "Where can we buy bread to feed all these people?" ⁶ He was testing Philip, for he already knew what he was going to do. ⁷ Philip replied, "Even if we worked for months, we wouldn't have enough money to feed them!" ⁸ Then Andrew, Simon Peter's brother, spoke up. ⁹ "There's a young boy here with five barley loaves and two fish. But what good is that with this huge crowd?" ¹⁰ "Tell everyone to sit down," Jesus said. So, they all sat down on the grassy slopes. (The men alone numbered about 5,000.) ¹¹ Then Jesus took the loaves, **gave thanks** to God, and distributed them to the people. Afterward he did the same with the fish. And they all ate as much as they wanted. ¹² After everyone was full, Jesus told his disciples, **"Now gather the leftovers, so that nothing is wasted."** ¹³ So they picked up the pieces and filled twelve baskets with scraps left by the people who had eaten from the five barley loaves. ¹⁴ When the people saw him do this miraculous sign, they exclaimed, "Surely, he is the Prophet we have been expecting!" ¹⁵ When Jesus saw that they were ready to force him to be their king, he slipped away into the hills by himself.*

PRACTICES:

1. Be Grateful to God for what you have right now.
2. Be Grateful to God for the lives you can help with what you have.
3. Be Grateful to God that nothing will go waste in your life.

CONCLUSION

Love is Grateful, so let us never forget the facts of gratitude and always follow the example of Jesus.

Small Group Lesson: UNDERSTANDING THE IMPORTANCE OF GRATITUDE—THE JESUS EXAMPLE (PART 2)

14 Make thankfulness your sacrifice to God, and keep the vows you made to the Most High. 15 Then call on me when you are in trouble, and I will rescue you, and you will give me glory." Psalm 50:14-15.

INTRODUCTION – If you can be grateful to God for where you came from and for where you are, no devil can stop you from seeing your God given dreams come to pass! If you can be grateful, no devil can stop your destiny! If you can be grateful, nothing can prevent you from seeing your God. Gratitude is the confidence of access into God's Presence and is a spiritual exercise and discipline that is filled with blessings of God.

DISCOVERY QUESTIONS

1. From the introduction, we know that Gratitude is the confidence of access into God's presence. How does gratitude grant us access into God's presence?

2. Why is Gratitude considered as a Spiritual Exercise and Discipline, and why does God bless those who express gratitude?

3. According to **Matt 11:25**, **Luke 10:22** and **Matt 15:36**, How did Jesus exemplify or show an example of gratitude?

4. In **John 11:41** and **Luke 22:17-18**, Why did Jesus always Thank the Father before performing miracles, sharing wine or breaking bread?

5. As a Child of God, what are some of the things God has done in your life that you are most thankful for? In what way can we express our thanksgiving?

PRACTICE FOR THE WEEK

1. Be grateful to God for knowing Jesus as your Lord and Saviour.
2. Be grateful for the ability to repent and turn to God.
3. Be grateful for the honour you will receive in heaven.

RESPOND IN PRAYER

1. Father in the name of Jesus, I proclaim that there is no one like You even among the gods. You are Glorious In Holiness and Fearful In Praises. Oh God. Accept my praises and thanksgiving in Jesus name.

2. Father, I thank you for the grace to be alive and to sing your praises to you today in Jesus name.
3. Oh Lord, I join the congregation of brethren to give praises to you for you have done great things in my life and in the church in Jesus name.
4. Oh Lord, I will praise you because you have delivered me from the hands of my enemies in Jesus name.

18

LOVE IS GRATEFUL (PART 3)— UNDERSTANDING THE IMPORTANCE OF GRATITUDE: THE JESUS EXAMPLE

If you can be grateful to God for where you came from and for where you are, no devil can stop you from seeing your God giving dreams come to pass! If you can be grateful, no devil can stop your destiny! If you can be grateful, nothing can prevent you from seeing your God.

OUTLINE

1. Facts about Gratitude:
2. The Practice of Gratitude

PURPOSE

Be encouraged to follow the example of Jesus in all seasons, situations, and circumstances to be grateful to God.

FACTS ABOUT GRATITUDE

1. Until God is shown gratitude for what He did for you in the past, He is not interested in what you want Him to do for you in the present and the future. **To attract God's interest in you, be grateful.**

2. Gratitude is the doorway to the destiny of glory (Jer. 30:19; Rom. 8:29-20; Prov. 3:35)

3. The believer's destiny of glorification is feasible by the action of his gratitude (Rom. 8:29-20). **To be glorified, be grateful.**

4. Gratitude is the escape route from the world of smallness to the world of greatness. **To be Great, be grateful.**

5. Gratitude secures one's past, and present blessings, and attracts his future blessings (Mal. 2:1-4; Dan. 4:34-35, 37). **To secure and attract God's blessings be grateful.**

THE PRACTICE OF GRATITUDE

1. Before raising Lazarus from the dead (Jn 11:1-14, 38-41).

Now a man named Lazarus was sick. He was from Bethany, the village of Mary and her sister Martha. ² (This Mary, whose brother Lazarus now lay sick, was the same one who poured perfume on the Lord and wiped his feet with her hair.) ³ So the sisters sent word to Jesus, "Lord, the one you love is sick."

⁴ When he heard this, Jesus said, "This sickness will not end in death. No, it is for God's glory so that God's Son may be glorified through it." ⁵ Now Jesus loved Martha and her sister and Lazarus. ⁶ So when he heard that Lazarus was sick, he stayed where he was two more days, ⁷ and then he said to his disciples, "Let us go back to Judea."

⁸ "But Rabbi," they said, "a short while ago the Jews there tried to stone you, and yet you are going back?" ⁹ Jesus answered, "Are there not twelve hours of daylight? Anyone who walks in the daytime will not stumble, for they see by this world's light. ¹⁰ It is when a person walks at night that they stumble, for they have no light."

¹¹ After he had said this, he went on to tell them, "Our friend Lazarus has fallen asleep; but I am going there to wake him up." ¹² His disciples replied, "Lord, if he sleeps, he will get better." ¹³ Jesus had been speaking of his death, but his disciples thought he meant natural sleep.

¹⁴ So then he told them plainly, "Lazarus is dead, ¹⁵ and for your sake I am glad I was not there, so that you may believe. But let us go to him." ¹⁶ Then Thomas (also known as Didymus) said to the rest of the disciples, "Let us also go, that we may die with him."

³⁸ Jesus, once more deeply moved, came to the tomb. It was a cave with a stone laid across the entrance. ³⁹ "Take away the stone," he said. "But, Lord," said Martha, the sister of the dead man, "by this time there is a bad odor, for he has been there four days." ⁴⁰ Then Jesus said, "Did I not tell you that if you believe, you will see the glory of God?"

⁴¹ So they took away the stone. Then Jesus looked up and said, "Father, I thank you that you have heard me. ⁴² I knew that you always hear me, but I said this for the benefit of the people standing here, that they may believe that you sent me."

⁴³ When he had said this, Jesus called in a loud voice, "Lazarus, come out!" ⁴⁴ The dead man came out, his hands and feet wrapped with strips of linen, and a cloth around his face. Jesus said to them, "Take off the grave clothes and let him go."

How?

- Be grateful to God for friends and family in difficult times.
- Be grateful to God and stand with family and friends going through difficult times.
- Be grateful to God for your family and friends to the end.

Who do you need to show gratitude to today? Think about two or three people to help.

2. Before sharing wine at the Passover meal (Lk 22:17-18). Before breaking bread (Lk 22:19), and sharing wine (Mt 26:27; Mk 14:23) at The Last Supper.

*22 Now the Festival of Unleavened Bread, called the Passover, was approaching, ² and the **chief priests and the teachers of the law** were looking for some way to get rid of Jesus, for they were afraid of the people. ³ Then **Satan entered Judas**, called Iscariot, one of the Twelve. ⁴ And Judas went to **the chief priests and the officers of the temple guard** and discussed with them how he might **betray***

Jesus. *⁵ They were delighted and agreed to give him money. ⁶ He consented and watched for an opportunity to hand Jesus over to them when no crowd was present.*

The Last Supper

⁷ Then came the day of Unleavened Bread on which the Passover lamb had to be sacrificed. ⁸ Jesus sent Peter and John, saying, "Go and make preparations for us to eat the Passover."

⁹ "Where do you want us to prepare for it?" they asked.

¹⁰ He replied, "As you enter the city, a man carrying a jar of water will meet you. Follow him to the house that he enters, ¹¹ and say to the owner of the house, 'The Teacher asks: Where is the guest room, where I may eat the Passover with my disciples?' ¹² He will show you a large room upstairs, all furnished. Make preparations there."

¹³ They left and found things just as Jesus had told them. So, they prepared the Passover.

¹⁴ When the hour came, Jesus and his apostles reclined at the table. ¹⁵ And he said to them, "I have eagerly desired to eat this Passover with you before I suffer. ¹⁶ For I tell you, I will not eat it again until it finds fulfillment in the kingdom of God."

¹⁷ After taking the cup, he gave thanks and said, "Take this and divide it among you. ¹⁸ For I tell you I will not drink again from the fruit of the vine until the kingdom of God comes."

¹⁹ And he took bread, gave thanks, and broke it, and gave it to them, saying, "This is my body given for you; do this in remembrance of me."

²⁰ In the same way, after the supper he took the cup, saying, "This cup is the new covenant in my blood, which is poured out for you. ²¹ But the hand of him who is going to betray me is with mine on the table. ²² The Son of Man will go as it has been decreed. But woe to that man who betrays him!"

HOW?

- Be grateful to God when you are not too sure of the people you are dealing with.
- Be grateful to God when you are faced with betrayal.
- Be grateful to God when you are faced with death.
- Be grateful in trusting God through your difficult times.

CONCLUSION

We must be grateful to God by looking at the facts of gratitude and seriously follow the example of Jesus's lifestyle of gratitude.

Small Group Lesson: UNDERSTANDING THE IMPORTANCE OF GRATITUDE—THE JESUS EXAMPLE (III)

"Unto thee, O God, do we give thanks, unto thee do we give thanks: for that thy name is near thy wondrous works declare" - **Psalm 75:1.**

INTRODUCTION -No duty is more urgent than giving thanks. Gratitude turns what we have into enough, and more. It turns denial into acceptance, chaos into order, confusion into clarity. It makes sense of our past, brings peace for today, and creates a vision for tomorrow. Jesus being God and man, was grateful to the father, to be an example to us. Let's be Grateful to God

LESSON OBJECTIVE

To Be encouraged to follow the example of Jesus in all seasons, situations, and circumstances to be grateful to God.

Scripture Reading - John 11:1-14, 38-41 | Luke 22:19-20

DISCOVERY QUESTIONS

1. Why did Jesus wait for 4 more days after the death of Lazarus before visiting to raise him up? *~John 11:4*

2. How should our attitude towards God be, when we feel he has delayed in raising up our Lazarus back to life? ~ *Habakkuk 3:17-18*

3. When Jesus came to Lazarus' tomb, he was told the body stinks by now but, after Jesus gave thanks to God in prayer, Lazarus was resurrected back to life. What can we learn from Jesus' example? ~ *John 11: 41-42*

4. At the Lord supper in *Luke 22: 19-20*, Jesus knew the suffering and the cruel death that was ahead of him, but he took the bread and the cup and gave thanks to the father. How can we also be grateful and thank God we go through pain and suffering? ~ *Hebrew 12:2*

PRACTICE FOR THE WEEK

1. Be Grateful to God for friends and family in difficult times.
2. Be Grateful in trusting God through your difficult times.
3. Be Grateful to God when you are faced with betrayal.

RESPOND IN PRAYER

1. Father in the Name of Jesus, help me to be thankful and to praise you even when am going through difficulties, knowing that all things work together for the good to them that love the Lord.

2. Father, I thank you for the lives of my family, friends and loved ones. May you cause them to rejoice and praise you in their sufferings, and help them to know that suffering produces perseverance, perseverance, character, and character produces hope in Jesus's name.

THE LOVE SERMONS

.

Conclusion

Thank you for reading, meditating, and applying the messages. You can please feel free to adapt it for your use to be a blessing to the body of Christ. Look out for **The Love Sermons, Volume 2.**

Love loves. So, love as God your Father loves.

www.ingramcontent.com/pod-product-compliance
Lightning Source LLC
LaVergne TN
LVHW051054080426
835508LV00019B/1869